WHAT TO EAT NOW
SPRING & SUMMER

WHAT TO EAT NOW

SPRING & SUMMER

THE BEST OF SPRING AND SUMMER EATING

VALENTINE WARNER

PHOTOGRAPHS BY HOWARD SOOLEY

MITCHELL BEAZLEY

CONTENTS

INTRODUCTION

The swallows are back, looping joyfully in their fly-catching pursuits to feed their demanding children, and the gentle daybreak cooings of the wood pigeon are met with smiles from the pillow. Country lanes are thick with the pong of wild garlic and village greens smell pleasantly of sweet mown cuttings. Cows let out from overwintering go bonkers in their crazy moment of release, as if trying to throw phantom rodeo riders, while blind newborns wobble in the trees and fields. Once more I can excitedly regiment my fly boxes as the rivers wake up and now my gun is locked away and replaced with my obsession for fishing.

I love my jumper collection, but – yippee! – summer's coming. As spring turns everything greener, one must strike like a kingfisher at the short seasonal ins and outs. Heavy raids on purple sprouting broccoli become leaping grabs at the elderflowers. Native molluscs are better left closed, but meanwhile the bass, mackerel and bream flash around over grumpy fat lobsters, hunting their targets into warmer, shallower waters.

May sees erotic asparagus charging up through the soil, then bowing to the arrival of regal artichokes, as herbs stand close to sunlit walls, waiting to add their flair. July is a blood-letting of red fruits, as juices stain the fingers and chins in the race to get there before the blackbird's beak. Fat-bottomed tomatoes threaten to snap their branches in humid hothouses, as the samphire becomes woody on the shores and the last adorable broad bean has been popped from its furry pod. Meat benefits from the rich grasses of late spring and summer, with excellent beef to lay over the pulsing white embers of the barbecue, and good milk squirts from the teat.

Throughout these 6 months the abundance becomes generous beyond belief and a Continental approach to food shopping – that is, outdoors and giving everything a good squeeze – really illustrates the arrival and departure of our wonderful fare.

As for this book, although not in itself edible, which might come in handy during a credit crunch, it aims to feed you through this clement time with recipes to freshen your spirit, lighten your step and engage you in joyful cooking, as the clink of glasses and happy chat drift through the kitchen window from outside. This is not a time for the slow, sturdy dishes of autumn and winter, so the following recipes are written with that in mind. Although preparation should always be undertaken with summer loving and in the time needed, our seasonal urge is to be out and about whenever possible. It's time for lazy picnics in the bluebells, chicken leg in hand and clouds trundling overhead, and salad lunches with good things peeking out from behind fresh leaves like wildlife in the hedgerows. There are simple things that need no complication, for those desperate to get an evening session in the pub, and clean breakfasts now that egg, sausage and a fried slice are inappropriate. Find sumptuous fruit puddings, chilled ices to give you a head cramp and soothing evening coolers to sip in the dying light.

And of course quite a number of recipes are dedicated to cooking over wood, as now is the time for tong masters and prodding commanders to take the barbecue helm. Here I offer delightful alternatives to blackened sausages, distressed burgers and curiously raw chicken.

I hope there is plenty in here you will like and preferably eat outside, with condensation running down a bottle of something good (but then again it will probably be pissing with rain).

SIRLOIN WITH CHIMICHURRI SAUCE

I have splashed, daubed, painted and dobbed all sorts of sauces, dips, marinades, cures and unctions over the noble beef sirloin, but the discovery of chimichurri was a true revelation – and no wonder, it coming from a land whose currency is beef. I have never travelled in Argentina, but with some research, foreign calls and good advice I feel that this recipe can rightfully call itself chimichurri and stand as proud as the gauchos of the Pampas.

Serves 8–10

1 x 2kg boned well-hung beef sirloin,
    not rolled
flaked sea salt and ground black pepper

CHIMICHURRI SAUCE
10–12 garlic cloves

2–3 long red chillies
2 large handfuls of fresh young
    curly parsley
4 heaped teaspoons dried oregano
2 teaspoons flaked sea salt
5 tablespoons red wine vinegar
4–5 tablespoons virgin olive oil
5 tablespoons cold water

To make the chimichurri sauce, first peel the garlic and deseed the chillies. Chop both very finely and scoop into a clean jam jar. Remove the tough stalks from the parsley and finely chop the leaves. Add the parsley leaves to the jar along with the oregano, salt, vinegar, oil and water. Stir until all the ingredients are well combined. Put the lid on and leave to sit for several hours or overnight, allowing the flavours to develop.

Roughly 1½ hours before serving, light the barbecue, making sure that you use enough coals to maintain a good temperature for at least an hour. Season the beef all over with salt and a few twists of black pepper.

When the coals are dusted with a fine coating of grey ash and all the flames have gone (this is essential, as otherwise the meat will burn) – after about 30 minutes – put the beef on a rack over the top so that the meat is around 25cm from the coals. Sear on the fatty side until well coloured, then cook fat-side up for 25 minutes. Turn the sirloin again before cooking for a further 20 minutes. Ideally, the barbecue lid should be on and the vents open. When the beef is done, lift on to a board and leave to rest for 10 minutes.

Carve the beef into thick slices. Give the sauce a good shake and spoon it over the beef as it is served. Fried potatoes with a tomato and onion salad (*see* page 157) would be spot-on.

STEAK TARTARE

The mere sight of fillet steak sitting raw on a plate is enough to make me pounce across the room and fall snarling on top of it, then gulp it down with bared teeth and rolling eyes. But that lacks etiquette, so in more refined moments I like to make a steak tartare.

Serves 1

100g good beef fillet steak
1 smallish shallot
2 small gherkins, drained
1 good teaspoon chopped chervil leaves
1 tablespoon baby capers, drained
flaked sea salt

1 medium free-range egg

SEASONING
any combination of the following, to
    taste: tomato ketchup, Worcestershire
    sauce, Tabasco sauce, Dijon mustard,
    ground white pepper

Trim the steak of any excess fat or sinew, and cut the meat into tiny pieces about the size of the small gobbets that eagle chicks are fed by their parents, or the smallest you can manage. Put in a neat pile in the centre of a refined plate. Depress a little crater in the top. Peel and very finely chop the shallot. Very finely chop the gherkins and chervil. Teeny-weeny is what you are after; the point of the dish is finesse. Place in small piles around the steak, along with the capers and a wee mound of salt.

Carefully crack the egg with a hard tap on the side of a bowl. Pass the yolk back and forth between the shell halves, allowing the egg white to drop into a container below, as white can come in handy for other recipes. (If kept only to dutifully make one meringue, don't feel too guilty about throwing it away.) Gently tip the yolk into the depression you made in the chopped steak.

It is time to decide which condiments will join the blend. My preferences are as follows, blobbed on top before forking in: 1 level teaspoon tomato ketchup, a dash of Worcestershire sauce, a dash of Tabasco sauce, ½ teaspoon Dijon mustard and a good pinch of white pepper. Mix everything on the plate together very thoroughly, really savouring the moment when you pop the yolk.

Eat alone and smile at life.

BARBECUED BAVETTE STEAK WITH ANCHOVIES, RED WINE AND GARLIC

This is a French cut of meat that in Britain would be the skirt nearer the hind leg. Flavoursome, juicy and tender, it is reasonably priced and perfect for casting on to the glowing grey and orange embers of a barbecue. The marinade has serious attitude and is not for wimps. This is my favourite preparation of beef when cooking outside.

Serves 4

5 sprigs of rosemary
1 large bulb of good hard garlic
2 tablespoons olive oil
100g anchovies in olive oil, drained
1 good tablespoon Dijon mustard
½ x 75cl bottle Côtes du Rhône red wine
a heavy blast of ground black pepper
finely grated rind and juice of 1 large
    unwaxed or well-scrubbed lemon
1 x 1kg beef skirt (bavette cut)

Strip the leaves off the rosemary. Peel and chop the garlic with the leaves and do not rest until all is microscopically fine. In a frying pan, heat the olive oil with the anchovy fillets over a medium heat. They will start to spit and when stirred with a wooden spoon will collapse. At this point add the garlic and rosemary, and continue to fry gently for a minute or so while keeping everything moving. The garlic should not colour. Stir in the mustard, wine, pepper and everything to do with the lemon. Try not to use that pot of grey-brown mustard that's half empty with a grizzled lid; you need good fresh stuff.

Turn down the heat and let everything simmer until you are left with about half the liquid. Allow the marinade to cool. Cut the beef into 2 pieces and put in a large ceramic or glass dish. Pour over the marinade and mix all together thoroughly. Cover and leave in the fridge for a minimum of 2 hours, but no more than 4, turning once or twice.

Light the barbecue 30 minutes before you want to start cooking. When the flames from your barbecue have died and the white coals are pulsing out their intense heat, cast on the bavette. Don't go prodding at it in that outdoor-cooking male way; just leave it for 3 minutes or so (more for well done) before turning it over. Paint over a little more mix on the cooked side and after 2 more minutes flip it again for 30 seconds or so. It is best cooked medium to rare. Rest for 4–5 minutes before carving at a slight angle. Serve with the rest of the wine, some good crusty bread, salad and a jar of Dijon mustard.

VEAL WITH MORELS AND MARSALA

Finding the magical spring morel in English woods delivers the same feelings to me as landing a big wild trout – pride, triumph, a joy in the chest, the urge to run home. But they are elusive, and so, unless you know of a closely guarded spot or a good grocer, use dried morels, which require no more than a foraging expedition to your local deli.

Serves 6

24 dried morel mushrooms (or equivalent amount of fresh)
1 bulb of new-season garlic or other good garlic
1 x 700g rose veal fillet, trimmed

flaked sea salt and ground black pepper
50g fridge-cold butter
1 tablespoon sunflower oil
100ml Marsala
juice of ½ medium lemon
1½ tablespoons chopped tarragon

If using fresh morels you will need a little stock in place of the liquor from soaking the dried morels. Steep the dried morels in boiling water until just covered and leave to swell. Break the garlic into individual cloves and peel. Tie the veal neatly with kitchen string in thumb-width intervals down its length – this will help form it into a compact shape for even cooking. Cut into 2 equal-sized pieces and season all over with salt and a few twists of black pepper.

Heat half the butter and the oil in a large, shallow lidded pan over a medium heat. Remember to return the remaining butter to the fridge, as it must be cold when you call upon its services again. When the butter has melted, turn up the heat. Be sure the butter is hot, as the veal should brown as quickly as possible; sitting in a puddle of butter without a sizzle or a spit is a pathetic vision and will ruin the overall cooking time. Brown the veal in the pan for a few minutes, turning every now and then until rich golden brown. Remove from the pan and put to one side.

Lift the morels from their liquor and give them a gentle squeeze. Keep the liquor. Add the garlic and morels to the butter and fry for 4–5 minutes, tossing regularly, until the garlic is golden brown. Add the Marsala to the pan, followed by the morel liquor, which should be poured through a sieve to exclude any grit. Reduce the liquid by half by boiling rapidly over a high heat.

Return the veal to the pan, cover with a lid and cook over a low heat for about 15 minutes, turning once or twice, until the veal is just firm on the outside but tender, pink and juicy within. Lift the veal from the pan, set it on a plate to rest and snip off the string. Turn up the heat to high again so that the sauce simmers and whisk the lemon juice into the pan, followed by the remaining butter, popped into the pan in small, cold pieces and whisked vigorously.

Cut the veal into slices the thickness of a draughts piece (about 1cm) and arrange them in some orderly assembly in the pan with the sauce. Scatter over with the tarragon and serve faster than immediately.

PORK & HAM

MAILLE MACRATO

Maille tonnato, or pork with tuna mayonnaise, may sound downright weird to many, but I tell you it is delicious! Delicious to the point that, were 100 people to be selected at random to try this dish, I really can't imagine more than 1 uttering: 'Ooh, no, it's yucky!' With so many mackerel zipping around our coastline, and with it being of the same family as tuna, I have replaced the tuna and subsequently the recipe name.

Serves 4

a few good sprigs of fresh thyme
1 x 600g boned pork loin
rind of 1 unwaxed or well-scrubbed lemon
flaked sea salt and ground black pepper
1 tablespoon olive oil, plus more to finish
 the dish
12 good-quality pickled white anchovies
 in oil, drained
2 tablespoons baby capers, drained
a squeeze of lemon juice

MACKEREL MAYONNAISE
1 medium mackerel, gutted and degilled
2 medium very fresh free-range egg yolks
1½ heaped teaspoons Dijon mustard
juice of ½ lemon
1 teaspoon flaked sea salt
a couple of twists of ground black pepper
50ml extra virgin olive oil
150ml sunflower oil
a dash of warm water (approx. 20ml),
 if needed

Preheat the oven to 190°C/375°F/Gas 5. Strip the leaves from the thyme and finely chop them. Remove the rind from the pork and roll the revealed fat in a mixture of the thyme leaves, grated lemon rind, salt and pepper. Put the handsome loin in a roasting tin and trail over the 1 tablespoon olive oil.

Before roasting the pork, place the unseasoned mackerel on an oven tray and bake for 10 minutes. Remove, put to one side and replace in the oven with the pork. Cook the meat for 40–60 minutes until just cooked but still ever so slightly pink on the inside. Leave to cool.

While the meat cooks, set about the rest of the mackerel mayonnaise. Drop the egg yolks, mustard, lemon juice, salt and pepper in a high-sided bowl. Whizz with a stick blender while slowly dribbling in the oils together until you have a consistency that holds its own without being too rigidly stiff. If the mayonnaise has become too thick, and there is still oil to add, just add a tablespoon of warm water before continuing with the oil. (If the mayo splits, do not throw it away, but start again with 1 egg yolk before incorporating back into the disaster you created before.)

When the mackerel is cold, carefully peel off the skin and remove the fillets from either side of the spine. Finely flake the fish into a bowl, stir in 5 tablespoons of the mayonnaise and mix well.

GOAT

CARNIVAL GOAT CURRY

Goat is a fabulous meat and woefully ignored. Certainly the Indian, African and Caribbean communities are wisely tucking in, but this country as a whole hasn't yet developed a taste for it. The last weekend of August sees the Notting Hill Carnival erupt on my doorstep and for me it's almost more about the goat than the music. If you still don't want to give it a try, replace goat with mutton. You are most likely to find both of them in Halal butchers.

Serves 8–10

2kg boned leg or shoulder of goat or mutton, trimmed and cut into 5cm pieces
6 fat garlic cloves, peeled and finely sliced
6 fresh bay leaves
2 cinnamon sticks
10 black peppercorns
2 teaspoons mild curry powder
1 teaspoon ground allspice
½ teaspoon ground cloves
¼ nutmeg, finely grated

1–2 Scotch bonnet chillies or 1–2 long red chillies, trimmed and chopped (with seeds)
5 tablespoons malt vinegar
roughly 6 tablespoons sunflower oil
2 large onions
2 x 400g tins chopped tomatoes
1 heaped tablespoon flaked sea salt
1 heaped tablespoon dark muscovado sugar
1 tablespoon black treacle
150ml cold water

Put the meat in a large bowl and add the garlic, bay leaves, cinnamon, peppercorns, curry powder, allspice, cloves, nutmeg and chillies. Rub the spices into the pieces of meat with 3 tablespoons of the vinegar. Cover and leave to marinate in the fridge for at least 3 hours and up to 12.

Preheat the oven to 170°C/325°F/Gas 3. Heat 2 tablespoons of the oil in a large frying pan and fry the meat with the garlic and spices in 3 or 4 batches until the meat is browned on all sides, adding more oil when necessary. Do not allow the garlic to burn. Transfer the meat and garlic to a large, lidded flameproof casserole. Peel and slice the onions. Add a little more oil to the frying pan and cook the onions until softened and lightly coloured. Tip them into the casserole. Deglaze the frying pan with the remaining malt vinegar, stirring to lift the sediment from the bottom; pour over the meat. Add the tomatoes, salt, sugar, treacle and water. Bring to the boil.

Cover with a lid and transfer to the oven. Cook for 2–2½ hours until the meat is very tender. Serve with rice that has been boiled, then fried with a little onion and some cooked black-eyed or red kidney beans. It is imperative that the curry be served with good and violent chile sauce and cans of ice-cold lager.

LAMB

ROLLED SHOULDER OF LAMB WITH PEPPER AND PINE NUT STUFFING

Very tasty indeed.

Serves 6

1 x 2kg boned lamb shoulder
a little olive oil
1 long sprig of rosemary
flaked sea salt and ground black pepper

STUFFING
2 large red peppers

2 large yellow peppers
100g pine nuts
3 tablespoons olive oil
100g day-old baguette
5 bushy sprigs of marjoram
4 fat garlic cloves
1 large unwaxed or well-scrubbed lemon
flaked sea salt and ground black pepper

To make the stuffing, put the peppers on a baking tray and place under a preheated hot grill close to the heat. Turn every now and again with tongs until the pepper skins are completely blackened and blistered. Transfer to a bowl. Cover with clingfilm and leave to cool for 15 minutes. When the peppers are ready to handle, strip off the skins with your fingers and discard. Open the peppers carefully and flick away the seeds. Do not do any of the above under running water, as you will wash away the delicious charred taste. Tear the flesh into long strips and put them in a large bowl.

Put the pine nuts in a dry frying pan. Toast over a medium heat until golden brown, turning occasionally. Watch like a hawk, as they are quick to burn. Tip them into the bowl with the peppers. Heat the oil in the same pan. Slice the bread, crusts and all, and cut it into small pieces roughly the dimensions of travel dice (½cm-ish). Scatter the bread into the frying pan and cook over a low heat until golden, stirring often. Add to the bowl with the peppers. Strip the marjoram leaves from the sprigs and finely chop. Peel and finely chop the garlic. Add these to the bowl as well. Grate the lemon rind over and season with plenty of salt and a few twists of black pepper. Mix well.

Place the lamb on a large board, skin-side down. Trim off any hard lumps of fat or sinew. It's now your job to make it into a neatish rectangle shape. Take a sturdy rolling pin and bash the thickest parts of the meat to flatten them, until the meat is 3–4cm thick. Trim off any untidy pieces and use them to patch holes or crevices; fill areas where the meat is more sparse. You are trying to create an even blanket of lamb on which to place the filling.

Twist the board so that one of the short sides of the lamb rectangle is closest to you. Squeeze the juice from the lemon over the lamb, flicking out any pips. Spoon the stuffing across the centre. Lift up the top and bottom of the lamb and wrap over the stuffing from both directions to make a fat parcel, with the pepper mixture just showing at both sides. Cut 7 lengths of kitchen string – each long enough to wrap around the lamb – and ease underneath the parcel, leaving 4cm between each one. Tie the strings very tightly, starting at each end, then the middle, then in between – this will help to keep the shape even. Trim off excess string. Push the stuffing in if it starts to escape. Finish by tying 1 long piece of string around the length of the lamb. Again trim off any excess string. Wrap the parcel tightly in a double layer of clingfilm and place in a small roasting tray or ovenproof dish. Cover and chill for 6 hours or overnight. Stand at room temperature for 30 minutes before roasting. (Ideally, this should be prepared the day before eating and left overnight to find its form.)

Preheat the oven to 190°C/375°F/Gas 5. Remove the clingfilm and weigh the lamb before returning it to the tin or dish. Rub it all over with olive oil. Chop the rosemary leaves very finely with a level tablespoon of flaked sea salt and a good grinding of pepper. Season the lamb well with most of this. Roast in the centre of the oven for 18–20 minutes per 500g stuffed weight. This will result in lamb that's a rich golden brown on the outside and nicely pink on the inside. Remove from the oven. Leave to rest for 10 minutes. Scatter with the remaining rosemary salt. Carve quite thickly and serve with fried potatoes, spinach and a good light red wine.

LAMB MEATBALLS WITH TOMATO SAUCE

A meatball should be succulent and giving, whether it is sitting in a nest of spaghetti or jammed in a crispy baguette with sauce dribbling out of the end. They should not bounce when thrown at the wall. In this recipe, I like to see them drowned in sauce.

Serves 6

2 large banana shallots
4 garlic cloves
2 tablespoons light olive oil, plus 3 more
    for frying the meatballs
2 stalks of rosemary
700g good lamb mince
freshly grated nutmeg
100g fresh white breadcrumbs
50ml whole milk
flaked sea salt and ground black pepper
lightly seasoned plain flour
extra virgin olive oil and Parmesan cheese,
    to serve

TOMATO SAUCE
1.2kg ripe tomatoes
1 tablespoon olive oil
300ml red wine
juice of 1 lemon
2 tablespoons tomato purée
2 level teaspoons flaked sea salt
1 teaspoon caster sugar
1 cinnamon stick

GREMOLATA
2 garlic cloves
a large handful of flat leaf parsley leaves
finely grated rind of 1 unwaxed or
    well-scrubbed lemon

To make the sauce, cut a small cross in the bottom of each tomato, then cut out and discard the stem bases. Place the tomatoes in a large mixing bowl. Pour over enough just-boiled water to cover and leave for 1 minute. Pour the water away and unrobe the loose skins from the flesh.

Chop the tomatoes in no particular fashion other than smallish. Put the oil in a large, shallow ovenproof casserole with a lid. You will know that the oil is hot enough when the tomatoes sizzle when added to the pan. Fry the tomatoes for 2–3 minutes until softened. Add the wine, lemon juice, tomato purée, salt and sugar. Bring to a gentle simmer and cook for 20 minutes.

While the sauce is simmering, preheat the oven to 170°C/325°F/Gas 3 and make the meatballs. Peel and finely chop the shallots and garlic, then fry them in the 2 tablespoons of olive oil until totally soft. Put in a large bowl. Strip the rosemary leaves from the stalks and chop them very finely. Add to the bowl along with the lamb mince, a good grating of nutmeg, the breadcrumbs and milk. Add plenty of salt and a few twists of black pepper. Use your hands to mix well.

It's worth frying a little of this mix before rolling it so that you can taste it and tweak the seasoning accordingly. When you are happy with the taste, roll the meatballs into about 24 balls between your palms, then roll lightly in seasoned flour. Fry over a high heat in the 3 tablespoons oil so that they brown quickly on all sides but remain raw in the middle. It is important during this stage that the oil is hot enough and that the meatballs are not all crammed together, so they fry well. Do in batches if necessary.

Nestle the meatballs together in the tomato sauce, add the cinnamon stick, cover with a lid and send to the oven for 1 hour. Remove from the oven and turn the meatballs over in the sauce. Return to the oven for a further 30 minutes. The meatballs should be very tender and the sauce rich.

Just before serving, make the gremolata. Peel and very finely chop the garlic, then put it in a small bowl. Finely chop the parsley and mix with the garlic and finely grated lemon rind. Scatter generously over the meatballs and sauce with a few splashes of extra virgin excellence to lift the whole dish into another dimension. A good teaspoon or 2 of Parmesan tapped over each bowl is welcome too.

LEFTOVERS: Warm the meatballs and stuff them with sauce into a lightly toasted baguette with American mustard, raw red onion and slices of tomato.

COCONUT LAMB

I can't remember how this came about other than a vague recollection of making it to take when camping at a musical festival. I seem to remember we forgot to eat it and barbecued it on our return. Be assured we had a very good cold box.

Makes 12 skewers (serves 6 as part
   of a barbecue)

1kg lamb neck fillet
150g sweetened desiccated coconut

MARINADE
1 small or ½ medium red onion, peeled
a good bunch of fresh coriander
2 garlic cloves, peeled
1 fat thumb of fresh root ginger, peeled
   and thickly sliced

1 long red chile, deseeded and
   thickly sliced
juice of 1 lime
2 tablespoons light muscovado sugar
6 cloves
1 teaspoon coriander seeds
1 tablespoon medium curry powder
1 heaped teaspoon ground turmeric
a good grating of nutmeg
1 tablespoon sunflower oil
½ teaspoon large flaked sea salt
1 x 440ml tin coconut milk

If using wooden skewers, pre-soak them prior to cooking, as this will help to prevent them from burning.

   First make the marinade. Roughly chop the onion and the coriander stalks and leaves. In a blender or food processor, blitz everything together except the coconut milk. Blend until the mixture is very well combined – you may need to remove the lid a couple of times and push the contents down with a spatula. Tip the marinade into a large shallow dish and add the coconut milk. Stir in thoroughly. Put to one side, covered, while the lamb is prepared.

   Put the lamb on a board and trim off any gnarly or unwanted pieces. Cut the lamb into diagonal slices roughly 2cm thick, then bash out each piece with your fist to flatten. Throw it into the marinade, making sure that all is combined well, and cover and chill for several hours.

   Double thread the meat lengthways on to the skewers. Sprinkle the desiccated coconut over a large plate. Take the skewers, one at a time, and roll in the coconut until evenly covered. Turn to coat a couple of times.

   Light the barbecue at least 30 minutes before you are ready to cook the lamb. When a thin layer of grey ash lightly covers the coals, it is time to cook. Place the lamb skewers on the barbecue close to the coals and cook for about 5 minutes on each side until golden and vaguely charred in places but tender and juicy within. (If the lamb starts to stick to the barbecue, cook on a piece of oiled foil.)

come in (hence the recipe's name), but unlike the US brown grocery bags our tiny brown-paper market bags are not as useful for degreasing chicken when it is popped inside. Serve hot with ketchup, mayonnaise or barbecue sauce and the French fries on page 182, followed by the raspberry ripple on page 232.

GUINEA FOWL: This recipe also works well with guinea fowl. Get the butcher to portion the guinea fowl for you, then follow the same method.

CHICKEN, HAM AND LEEK PIE

It's a terrible problem having one of these pies hanging around. Sitting there in the fridge it becomes a delicious diversion from work. Stupidly small slices demand an endless succession of sneaky trips to the kitchen until someone shouts: 'Hey, who ate all the pie?'

The only true place for this is on a picnic, where the whole lot gets eaten in one go. A lone picnic, of course.

Serves 10

PASTRY
400g plain flour, plus extra for dusting
½ teaspoon ground black pepper
50g fridge-cold butter, diced
175g fridge-cold lard, diced, plus a little
    extra for greasing the tin
150ml water
2 teaspoons flaked sea salt

GLAZE
15g lard, melted
1 free-range egg, beaten

FILLING
3 boneless good chicken breasts, skinned
200g hand-carved roast ham,
    thickly sliced
20 baby leeks, well washed and drained
25g fridge-cold lard, diced
1 teaspoon ground ginger
1 teaspoon ground mace
2½ teaspoons flaked sea salt
½ teaspoon ground black pepper
4 sheets of gelatine (about 8g)
250ml good fresh chicken stock

Cut each chicken breast in half lengthways and put in a large bowl. Cut the sliced ham into smallish pieces, about the size of an ordinary postage stamp. Trim the leeks and cut into roughly 3cm lengths. Add the ham and leeks to the chicken along with the diced lard, ginger, mace, salt and ground black pepper. Muddle together well, then put to one side while the pastry is made.

Grease a 17.5cm spring-clip cake tin with lard. To make the pastry, sift the flour into a large bowl and stir in the pepper. Rub in the butter and 50g of the lard until the mixture resembles fine breadcrumbs. Make a well in the centre. Put the water and salt in a small saucepan. Bring to a simmer, then remove from the heat and whisk in the remaining 125g lard. Pour this into the bowl with the flour. Stir well, first with a wooden spoon, then with your fingers, to make a smooth, pliable dough. Cover and leave for 15–20 minutes to allow it to become cool and workable.

Working quickly, reserve a third of the pastry to make a lid and roll out the remaining pastry on a heavily floured worksurface until around 5mm thick. Use this to line the cake tin, leaving around 3cm overhanging the edge. Press well into the base and side of the tin. Be very careful not to rip the pastry, as this will make it impossible to pour in the jelly later.

Spoon the chicken mixture into the pastry-lined tin, ensuring that the leeks and ham are dotted pretty evenly throughout. Don't pack everything in too tightly, as the jelly stock you'll be pouring in must be able to sneak its way round the entire interior.

Roll out the remaining pastry into a roughly 24cm round. Brush the overhanging edges of the pie with water and place the pastry lid on top. Press the edges firmly together to seal, then trim off most of the excess, leaving just enough to pinch into a neat crimped edge. Make a 1cm hole in the centre of the pastry lid. Place on a sturdy baking tray and chill for 30 minutes. Preheat the oven to 180°C/350°F/Gas 4.

Bake the pie in the centre of the oven for 1 hour. Take it out of the oven, very carefully release the sides of the tin and remove, but leave the base. Take great care not to crack the pastry, as this will be disastrous when it comes to pouring in the jelly. Return to the baking tray. Brush liberally with the melted lard for the glaze, then with some of the beaten egg, and continue baking for 15 minutes. Take out of the oven and brush with more egg. Return for a further 15 minutes until the pastry is crisp and golden brown. Leave to cool for 2–3 hours, putting in the fridge after the first hour.

To make the jellied stock, soak the gelatine sheets in a bowl of cold water for 5 minutes until softened. Heat the chicken stock in a small saucepan until it has just boiled, leave to cool slightly, then taste and tweak the seasoning, if needs be. Squeeze out the gelatine over the bowl, getting rid of the excess water, and drop it into the warm stock. Stir until completely dissolved, then transfer to a jug and leave to cool for 30 minutes. Do not allow it to set.

Using a funnel, pour the stock slowly into the pie, stopping every so often to wait for the liquid to trickle down between the layers. Halt when the stock reaches the top. Chill the pie for several hours or overnight until the stock jellifies.

Serve the pie in wedges with English mustard and chutney.

NOTE: If you can't get hold of baby leeks, use the slimmest leeks you can find. You'll need about 400g prepared weight.

CHICKEN LIVERS WITH BACON, PEAS AND MINT

I used to cook this in a west London restaurant. My approach would be to add a little more of everything than was needed for the portion. Then after the order was plated, I would eat the rest from the hot pan. This tended to infuriate the head chef, Toby – seeing me with gravy on my chin taking hurried mouthfuls as he called the next order. A good little meal when alone.

Serves 1

75g fresh podded peas
6 large chicken livers
50g rindless smoked streaky bacon
1 garlic clove
1 sprig of fresh thyme
a small handful of fresh mint leaves

½ tablespoon sunflower oil
flaked sea salt and ground black pepper
1 tablespoon sherry vinegar
4 tablespoons good chicken stock
1 teaspoon Dijon mustard
a good knob of fridge-cold butter, cut
    into small pieces

Bring a small saucepan of water to the boil. Add the peas and cook for 2 minutes. Drain in a sieve, then set aside. Trim the chicken livers, cutting out any sinew and unsightly bits.

As the rest of this recipe is so quick to cook, have all remaining ingredients that you will need standing to attention – a bit like cooking in a restaurant kitchen. If you don't, the chicken livers will overcook as you faff around; they should be just done, cooked to pink. Cut the bacon into thin strips (I like to buy bacon in 1 piece and cut little matchsticks, but you can also use rashers). Peel the garlic and chop finely. Strip the thyme leaves from the sprig and finely chop. Roughly tear the mint leaves.

Heat the oil in a small frying pan over a medium-high heat and fry the bacon for 3–4 minutes until beginning to colour. At this point, season the chicken livers with salt, ground black pepper and the thyme. Add them to the pan and fry until well coloured on one side – this should take around 30 seconds, providing the livers are sizzling the minute they hit the pan.

Flip the livers over and add the garlic. Cook for a few seconds so they colour on the other side, then shake the pan and toss everything around a little. Pour about the sherry vinegar to deglaze the pan and cook until it has almost evaporated. Add the peas, followed by the stock. Cook until the liquid has reduced by half.

Blob, then swirl in the mustard. Add the cold cubed butter and swirl the pan around until a glossy thickened sauce has formed. Spoon on to a soup plate, scatter with the torn mint and eat at once. Make sure that you have some good bread to chase the last of the tasty gravy around, or by all means lick the plate.

ROMAN CHICKEN LIVERS

There was a little restaurant in Rome where I used to go regularly with my father. I can remember only 3 things about it: 1. a stuffed boar's head that hung on the wall with a look not of ferocity but more comical surprise; 2. that the place was so dark in the evening, you could only just make out your white plate; 3. that we always ordered this delicious chopped liver served next to a dollop of mascarpone. When both were heavily loaded on to super-thin, crisped bread, it would snap and fall back on to the plate, leaving your empty mouth agape and a look rather like that of the boar on the wall. Here is a similar version with a more sensible bread.

Serves 4 as a pre-dinner steadier

250g good plump chicken livers
   (not frozen), well drained
½ small onion
2 small good, hard garlic cloves
20g butter
3 tablespoons extra virgin olive oil
a pinch of dried thyme
1 tablespoon good balsamic vinegar
1 tablespoon baby capers, drained

2 anchovy fillets in olive oil, drained
flaked sea salt and ground black pepper
125g mascarpone
flat breads (*see* page **200** for home-made)

TOMATO SALAD
16 cherry tomatoes
a handful of fresh basil
1 tablespoon extra virgin olive oil
flaked sea salt

If making your own flat breads, prepare the dough up to the point where it is risen and ready to cook (*see* page **200**).

Take each chicken liver and, with a small, sharp knife, cut out any sinew and unsightly bits from the centre. Pat them dry with kitchen paper and put to one side. Peel the onion and dice it very finely. Peel the garlic and chop it finely, keeping it separate from the onion.

Heat a frying pan with the butter and olive oil over a medium heat. Throw in the onion and thyme, and cook for 5 minutes or so until the onion is totally soft and golden. Add the garlic and stir. Clearing small spaces for the livers, settle them into the pan. Fry for 2 minutes on each side, until just pink. It is fine if the onion caramelises a little, but if you are concerned that it will burn stir around the livers. Splash over the vinegar and stir it a couple of times, then turn off the heat.

Transfer the livers immediately to a food processor with the baby capers and anchovies. Whizz until smooth. If you are using a blender, you will have to remove the lid from time to time and push everything back down towards the blades. Check the seasoning before flopping the mixture into a bowl.

For the salad, chop the tomatoes roughly into quarters and tear up the basil. Mix the 2 together in a bowl with the olive oil and salt to taste.

On a large plate, arrange the tomato salad with a very large dollop of the mascarpone and the small mountain of chicken livers, all in separate piles. Cook the bread (or warm up ready-made) and serve all together with a handful of knives. Attack.

GUINEA FOWL

Guinea fowl is widely available, but I would like to see it on more tables. The French, who have an enthusiastic hunger for this bird (or *pintard*, as they call it), also describe it as '*joli-laide*', as in 'ugly-beautiful'. Even with its blue-faced vulturine look, I think the guinea fowl is much more pretty than grotesque, in its beautiful spotted frock. But on being woken by their infernal dawn racket, one could only remark when seeing them sizzling through the oven door; 'they had it coming.'

I could say to those who have not tried guinea fowl the inevitable, 'it tastes rather like chicken,' but it is chicken with intrigue and definitely worth investigating for its pleasantly gamey taste. This bird, indigenous to Africa, responds well to unisons with ingredients such as fennel, Puy lentils and French mustard. Pretty much any method of cooking can be applied. It is delicious braised (very good with chicory), roasted or fried. But be careful when cooking guinea fowl, as although its legs are well fatted the high-arching and slim breast gives no lenience to overcooking.

GUINEA FOWL WITH FENNEL PURÉE

This velvety purée with crisp grilled guinea fowl on top is most delicious and quick to prepare.

Serves 2

1 guinea fowl
fine sea salt
sunflower oil

FENNEL PURÉE
2 large fennel bulbs

2 fat garlic cloves
2 tablespoons olive oil
40g butter
200ml white wine
2 tablespoons pine nuts
a squeeze of lemon juice
flaked sea salt and ground black pepper
50ml whole milk (optional)

Get your butcher to remove the breast and leg joints from a guinea fowl, or cut them off yourself as you would for a chicken (keep the carcass, as it makes good stock).

Trim the fennel and discard any damaged parts. Save any feathery fennel leaves for later. Cut the fennel into small pieces.

Peel the garlic and put it into a saucepan with the fennel, olive oil, butter and wine, then cover and cook at a gentle simmer until the fennel is very soft. This stage will take 30–40 minutes. Meanwhile, gently toast the pine nuts in a small, dry pan over a low to medium heat, moving them continually so that they don't burn, until they are golden brown. Remove the lid from the fennel pan and turn up the heat under the pan. Simmer hard until the wine has evaporated by half. Add a squeeze of lemon juice and season with salt and black pepper. Blitz in a food processor or with a stick blender until as smooth as possible; if you feel it is too thick, let it down with a little milk. Adjust the seasoning and stir in the chopped fennel leaves and the toasted pine nuts. The purée can now be reheated when needed.

Preheat the grill to high. Brush the skin of the guinea fowl generously with sunflower oil, and salt liberally. Lower into a flameproof frying pan over a medium heat so that when the meat enters the pan it sizzles immediately. Cook the guinea fowl (the breasts should be skin-side down) for 4 minutes until deep golden, regulating the heat so as not to burn it. Turn the breasts and legs over in their pan and immediately place under the grill for a further 8–10 minutes until tender but cooked. Remove from the heat. The skin should be crispy and a skewer inserted into the fattest part of the leg should seep clear juices.

Spoon the purée on to 2 warmed plates. Slice the breasts on a diagonal and place on top of the purée with the legs. Eat at once.

QUAILS

QUAILS WITH BRANDY

This nervous little bird, if offered a drink, would politely decline. But when not given the choice, the drunken quail is very agreeable company.

Serves 4

8 quails
2 sprigs of fresh thyme
1 sprig of rosemary

8 garlic cloves, peeled and thinly sliced
ground black pepper
250ml brandy
1½ tablespoons olive oil
flaked sea salt

Flatten the breastbone of each quail by leaning on them and exerting pressure with the palm of your hand. Turn each bird over and cut up each side of the backbone with strong kitchen scissors. Pull out the spine and discard or save for stock. Cut each bird in half from between the legs through to the neck. Put the birds in a bowl and add the stripped thyme leaves, rosemary, sliced garlic and 2 twists of black pepper. Steep everything in the brandy. Cover and leave in the fridge for at least 3 hours, turning occasionally.

Light the barbecue. When it glows with pulsing hot orange and white coals, rub the birds with the olive oil and season well. Thrust them on to skewers, 3 per skewer. As the sun fades, barbecue them in the evening light, turning often. After about 15 minutes they should be done; the juices should run clear when you push a knife into the thickest part of the thigh. Arrange on a plate and eat with paper napkins but without manners.

QUAILS WITH ROMESCO SAUCE

Whenever reaching for a quail, I cannot help but imagine myself as the hungry fairytale ogre terrorizing the locals. Each wee bird becomes a pleading villager about to be torn limb from limb, and in this case dipped in a giant's pot of romesco sauce. Nooo! Noooo! Scrunch.

Serves 3

6 quails
1–2 teaspoons sunflower oil
flaked sea salt and ground black pepper

ROMESCO SAUCE
2 red peppers

1 bulb of garlic
1 large beef tomato
3 tablespoons extra virgin olive oil
3 tablespoons flaked almonds
½ teaspoon smoked paprika
10g fresh white breadcrumbs
2 teaspoons sherry vinegar
flaked sea salt

To make the romesco sauce, first preheat the oven to 240°C/475°F/Gas 9. Cut the peppers in half and remove the seeds. Cut each half into 2 pieces and scatter over a baking tray. Cut the garlic bulb in half horizontally and add the bottom half (save the top for something else) to the peppers along with the tomato, cut into 4 wedges.

Pour 1 tablespoon of the oil over the vegetables and turn them lightly to coat. Send them to the oven and roast for 20 minutes. Remove the garlic and leave to cool. Continue roasting the peppers and tomato for a further 10 minutes. Exactly 5 minutes before removing them, slide a small sturdy baking tray sprinkled with the almonds into the oven and toast them to a rich golden colour. Remove the tomato, peppers and almonds from the oven.

Blitz the almonds and paprika in a food processor. Scrape the pepper flesh and tomatoes from their skins into the processor. Scoop the cooked garlic out of its skins and drop this in with the breadcrumbs, vinegar and remaining oil. Blend together well until as smooth as possible. You may need to remove the lid a couple of times to push the mixture down with a rubber spatula. Scrape the mixture into a bowl and season with plenty of salt. This sauce will certainly improve if it is made a day ahead and kept in the fridge until needed. Cover and leave to come to room temperature for about 30 minutes before serving.

Light the barbecue or preheat the grill. To prepare each quail, take a pair of scissors and, holding the bird breast-side down in the palm of your hand, cut out the spine and discard it. Now put the bird on a board, breast-side up, and flatten the breastbone by leaning on the bird and pressing down hard using the bases of your hands.

Rub the birds generously with the sunflower oil and season well with salt and black pepper. When the barbecue glows with pulsing hot and orange white coals, lay the quails, breast-side up, on the barbecue and cook relatively close to the coals for about 6 minutes. Turn them over and cook the breast side for about 8 minutes more, moving them strategically to a cooler place on the barbecue if burning. (If cooking the birds indoors, preheat the grill to medium. Sear the birds first, breast-side down, in a heatproof frying pan over a high heat until browned – 3–4 minutes. Put the pan under the grill and cook the back of the birds for about 5 minutes. Turn them over and finish cooking for another 3 minutes.) Whether cooked on the barbecue or grill, the quails' juices should run clear when you push a knife into the thickest part of a thigh.

Sit down to a small pile of tasty little birds smeared with plenty of sauce. Then lick your fingers like the ogre that has just eaten 6 farmers.

Val warner

FISH DISHES

TROUT, SEA TROUT & SALMON

When spoon and chopping board are not close to me, the river and rod invariably are; here I must remember that this is a cookery book, not a fishing book. All parts of finding the breakfast tiddler or wily hook-jaw, then catching them, offer as much pleasure to me as their preparation and eating. When fishing I am under the same spell as I am in the kitchen. All becomes guided by curious hunches, instinct and rule-breaking.

Britain is home to indigenous brown trout (closest to my heart) and the rainbow trout. The latter arrived here from the United States and, although mainly farmed now, also secretively breeds in a few particularly pretty rivers. Both are good, with firm and delicate-tasting flesh, except when taken from silted or muddy waters.

For me, the quintessential summer dish is cold trout with some new potatoes and herb mayonnaise – and of course smoked trout next to buttery scrambled eggs. Never forget the great fish cake (just hold back a bit on the potato). Tarragon grows for trout, and large sprigs of rosemary, burnt on the barbecue next to the sizzling fish, do something wonderful.

The sea trout is a browny that has boldly decided to go and seek its fortune in the oceans, leaving sweet water for salty adventure. No one knows why this happens, but some feel it mainly occurs in rivers with less natural food.

The salmon is a truly extraordinary fish, and catching it can be like playing darts blindfolded and standing on a giant spring. I rarely take either of these fish home, as their natural stocks are now seriously threatened. But this is not the place for an essay on the problems caused by salmon farming.

When buying wild salmon, be prepared for a sharp intake of breath on receiving the bill. If buying farmed, avoid fish that are very deep in body, with techno-orange-coloured flesh; they will be flabby, greasy and stuffed full of undesirables. Pointier tails can be a sign of less cramped conditions, and, although I am wary of the 'O' word, organic fish tend to be better than non.

To finish this introduction on a high note, I return to the river. As with cooking, when the trout rod is gripped in hand and the sun is dipping down, all the senses are on full alert. Fingers tremble as I tie a hasty fly; ears prick up for the sound of snatch or gulp after the careless beetle tumbles from his leaf; eyes look for shifting shadows in the current, or quiet rises beneath the willow. All around water rats, chin up, brave a swim above the shadowy pike, ducklings chase the upward snow-like blizzard of mayfly and the grey wagtail wobbles by the weir. It's not football, but fishing, that is the beautiful game.

TROUT CROQUETTES

During the summer, if not at home or work, I'll most likely be on a riverbank hunched over my fly box, hurriedly trying to find a suitable choice for a fussy trout. Even after I have slipped the majority back into the current, a lot of trout still come home with me, and this is my favourite pre-dinner trout snack.

Makes 15

1 x 450g fresh brown or rainbow trout, gutted and degilled
25g butter
½ small onion
40g plain flour
250ml whole milk
1 teaspoon tomato purée
2 teaspoons finely chopped fresh tarragon

1 teaspoon Dijon mustard
3 tablespoons double cream
flaked sea salt and ground black pepper
2 large free-range eggs
100g very fine breadcrumbs, made from dry white bread (*see* opposite)
8 tablespoons ground almonds
3 tablespoons plain flour
sunflower oil for deep-frying and oiling
lemon wedges for squeezing

Preheat the oven to 190°C/375°F/Gas 5. Place the trout on a baking tray lined with oiled foil. Cover with a second sheet of foil and bake for 12–15 minutes until it is just cooked. Allow the trout to cool. Discarding the skin, flake the fish into a sieve over a bowl. Do this carefully, being extra diligent to take out any tiny bones.

Melt the butter in a medium saucepan. Peel and finely chop the onion. Gently fry until pale golden. Stir in the 40g flour and cook for 30 seconds before gradually stirring in the milk. Cook over a low heat for 5 minutes, stirring constantly, until the sauce is glossy and thick. Beat in the tomato purée, tarragon, mustard, cream and plenty of salt and black pepper. Cover with clingfilm to prevent a skin forming, and allow to cool until tepid. Gently stir in the trout until thoroughly incorporated and adjust the seasoning to taste. Spoon the mixture into a bowl and cover again with clingfilm. Allow to cool. Cover and chill for a minimum of 5 hours or until solid.

When ready to cook, make croquettes using 2 dessertspoons to form the mixture into small ovals, then slightly ball between your palms. Beat the eggs well in a large bowl. Scatter half the breadcrumbs in a shallow bowl and mix with half the almonds. Put the 3 tablespoons flour in a third bowl.

Toss each croquette lightly in flour, then into the egg, before coating evenly in the breadcrumb mixture. Put on a small baking tray. After 8 croquettes have been prepared, tip out the used breadcrumbs (they will be sticky and lumpy) and replace them with the remaining breadcrumbs and almonds. Chill the croquettes for at least 30 minutes or until just before serving.

Half-fill a large pan with sunflower oil and heat to 180°C/350°F. Using a metal slotted spoon, carefully lower 5 croquettes at a time into the hot oil and cook for about 2½ minutes turning them once, until the coating is golden

and squeeze the whole lemon into it. Add the chile flakes, some salt and black pepper, and the extra virgin olive oil. Put the fish on a platter and lay the eggs, sliced in half and seasoned, next to it. Halve and season the tomatoes, placing them on the platter. Take the separate groups of vegetables 1 by 1, toss them in the bowl with the dressing and arrange them around the fish. Slice and dress the beetroot last, so as not to stain the other vegetables shocking pink. Carry the whole thing to the table and eat with greedy spoonfuls of the aïoli.

GRAVLAX

Give me cured fish, then give me more. The Scandinavians are the supreme masters of curing treatments. This recipe replaces white sugar with dark brown, as it makes for a deeper and more intriguing taste.

Makes 1.5kg (serves about 12)

90g flaked sea salt
60g dark muscovado sugar
1 level tablespoon ground
    white pepper
60g fresh dill
2 x 1kg sides of fresh salmon, scaled,
    filleted and pin-boned

DILL SAUCE
2 medium free-range egg yolks
2 tablespoons white wine vinegar
1 tablespoon German mustard
1 tablespoon caster sugar
200ml sunflower oil
3 tablespoons finely chopped fresh dill
flaked sea salt

Mix the salt, muscovado sugar and white pepper thoroughly. It may seem like a lot of pepper, but trust me. Strip the dill feathers, discarding the stalks, and chop them finely with a sharp knife. Mix in with the salt and sugar, but be ready to use it straight away, as ignored it will become wet and sticky.

Place 1 filleted fish half, skin-side down, in a large, shallow ceramic or glass dish. Scatter the dill mixture evenly over the salmon and place the other fillet on top, skin-side up. Cover with a piece of clingfilm and apply considerable weight in the form of 3 or 4 dinner plates or a few tins of unopened baked beans resting on a small tray. Leave for 2 days in the fridge. Turn the salmon over every 6 hours or so, spooning over some of the juice that collects below between the halves. Replace the clingfilm and weights each time. After 2 days, remove the salmon from the dish and pat it dry with kitchen paper. Discard the juices.

To make the dill sauce, put the egg yolks in a bowl and whisk in the vinegar, mustard and caster sugar. Gradually add the oil while beating vigorously with a whisk until the sauce is thick and glossy. This can be done in a blender, but if it becomes proud and thick like mayo, this is not right and you can let it down with a little warm water to the consistency of double cream. Stir in the dill and season with salt. Use a very sharp knife to cut the fillets diagonally towards the tail in thin slices. The thin end may be a little salty, but is good snipped into scrambled eggs. Serve with the dill sauce and rye bread.

MACKEREL

MACKEREL NIÇOISE

This reminds me of happy days in the South of France eating lunch on some harbour, looking at the boats from under the shade of an umbrella, drawing on the paper tablecloth and slowly becoming drowsy with little carafes of chilled white wine. Mackerel is an excellent replacement for tuna.

Serves 4

2 large mackerel, gutted and degilled
flaked sea salt and ground black pepper
1 tablespoon light olive oil
350g waxy new potatoes, eg Charlotte
    or Jerseys, well scrubbed
125g fine green beans, stalks trimmed
4 small free-range eggs (at room
    temperature)
8 good salted anchovy fillets in oil, drained
100g vine cherry tomatoes
1–2 Baby Gem lettuce
a handful of good black olives in oil,
    drained and pitted if preferred

2 tablespoons baby capers, drained
a handful of small fresh basil leaves

DRESSING
½ short stalk of rosemary
2 small free-range egg yolks
2 garlic cloves, peeled and
    roughly chopped
1 teaspoon Dijon mustard
1 tablespoon red wine vinegar
1 tablespoon freshly squeezed
    lemon juice
100ml light olive oil
a splash of hot water, if needed

Preheat the grill to full blast.

First make the dressing. Strip the leaves from the rosemary (you should be left with roughly a teaspoonful) and put in a blender with the egg yolks, garlic, mustard, vinegar and lemon juice. Blend until well combined, then slowly, in a thin dribble, add the oil. If the dressing appears too thick, add a splash of hot water and blend until the dressing reaches a double cream-like pouring consistency. Leave to one side while the other ingredients are prepared.

Place the mackerel, seasoned and lightly oiled, on a foil-lined grill tray. Grill for 4–5 minutes on each side until cooked. Allow to cool.

Cook the potatoes in a large saucepan of simmering water for about 15 minutes until tender, adding the beans for the last 5 minutes of cooking time. Drain in a colander, then immediately plunge into a large bowl of iced water and leave to cool completely.

Lower the eggs gently into another saucepan of boiling water. Return to the boil and cook for 8 minutes. Cool quickly under running water until cold. Peel the eggs and cut in half. They should be only just hard-boiled with the yolk moist and a rich golden-yellow colour.

Remove and discard the mackerel skin and take the flesh from the bones in nice large flakes. Be extra careful when extracting it, as it would be nice to eat the salad without regularly sticking your fingers in your mouth to remove the bones under cover of your napkin. Chuck the bones.

Drain the potatoes and cut into fairly thick slices. Cut the anchovies in half lengthways and the tomatoes through the middle. Roughly tear the lettuce leaves. Toss the mackerel pieces, potatoes, green beans, lettuce, anchovies, tomatoes, olives, capers and basil leaves loosely together in a large salad bowl. Put the halved eggs here and there before liberally spooning over the dressing. Eat with a cold bottle of rosé.

MACKEREL TATAKI

This is a fine way to approach small and lean summer mackerel. The tastes are so clean. If you carry a tiny case with the rapid response kit of ingredients, you can make this outdoors with fish caught or bought. Make sure that the fish is super-fresh.

Serves 2

2 teaspoons sesame seeds
1 medium very fresh mackerel, gutted
   and degilled
½ thumb of fresh root ginger

2 small spring onions
⅛ sheet of toasted Nori seaweed
   (optional)
2 teaspoons good Japanese soy sauce
1½ teaspoons sesame oil
a squeeze of lemon juice

In a small frying pan, toast the sesame seeds until light golden brown, then tip them out and leave them to cool. Fillet, de-bone and skin the fish. Removing the cellophane-thin skin of a mackerel can be tricky and, I must tell you, is not totally necessary, but it makes the dish that much better. Chop the fish into small pieces no bigger than Scrabble pieces and put them in the bowl you plan to eat from. Use a really sharp knife so that you are cutting the fish, not mashing it.

    Peel the ginger and chop it super-fine. Pull off the outer layer of the spring onions and trim any withered tops. Lay on their sides and cut into teeny-weeny rings. Really fine chopping is essential for the ginger and spring onions. Add the onions, ginger and sesame seeds to the fish. If using, cut the Nori in half. Place the squares on top of each other and snip some fine whiskers into the bowl.

    Mix all together with the soy sauce, sesame oil and a squeeze of lemon juice. Eat straight away with chopsticks, like a heron catching sticklebacks.

SARDINES

SARDINES WITH TAPENADE AND POTATOES

I ate this in one of the best towns in which one can eat, San Sebastian in Spain, known locally as Donostia. I managed to infiltrate a private men's dining club where lots of old dudes shuffled around a large kitchen all wearing glasses on a chain around their necks. Some of the 8 courses they prepared were delicious; some not. This was fantastic, but I still think it even better replacing the whole olives that they used with my tapenade.

Serves 2

350g large waxy new potatoes,
    eg Charlotte, well scrubbed
flaked sea salt
2 tablespoons olive oil, plus extra for
    grilling the sardines and to finish
    the dish
1 small or ½ medium red onion
8 spanking-fresh sardine fillets, scaled
    and gutted
ground black pepper

a handful of young thyme leaves
juice of ½ small lemon

TAPENADE
150g good black olives, pitted
6 anchovy fillets in olive oil, drained
2 garlic cloves, peeled and
    roughly chopped
15g Parmesan cheese, grated
1 heaped teaspoon baby capers, drained
a squeeze of lemon juice
3 tablespoons good olive oil

Bring a large saucepan of water to the boil. Add the potatoes and a good pinch of salt. Return to the boil. Cook for about 15 minutes until the potatoes are tender but firm. Meanwhile, make the tapenade. Put the olives, anchovies, garlic, Parmesan and capers in a food processor. Add the lemon juice and the oil. Blend until well combined – you may need to remove the lid and push the mixture down once or twice. Adjust the seasoning to taste.

Drain the potatoes in a colander, then put them under running water until cold. Peel them. Transfer to a board and cut into slices, lengthways, about the thickness of 2 stacked £1 coins, wetting the knife occasionally as this helps. Throw in a mixing bowl and drizzle with the olive oil. Peel and slice the onion into paper-thin rings. Mellow in a bowl of cold water. Put to one side.

Preheat the grill to high. Brush the skin side of the fish with olive oil and season with salt and a good grinding of black pepper. Grill for 4 minutes or until cooked. Arrange the potatoes, drained onions and hot sardines on a large plate. Spoon the tapenade about the dish. Scatter with thyme leaves and some coarsely ground black pepper. Add a dribble of olive oil. Squeeze over the juice from the half a lemon. Serve quickly before the sardines go cold.

SARDINES ESCABECHE

All things sweet and sour please me greatly. This treatment of sardines tastes so good and makes a very pretty dish when set down outdoors for summer lunch. There are 8 in the bed and the little one says, 'eat me.'

Serves 3–4

a big handful of sultanas
3 tablespoons plain flour
flaked sea salt and ground black pepper
5 tablespoons light olive oil
6–8 stiff fresh sardines, scaled, gutted
    and degilled
2 medium red onions
1 teaspoon cumin seeds

1 teaspoon coriander seeds
5–6 sprigs of fresh young thyme leaves,
    plus extra, to garnish
4 small bay leaves
2 big juicy oranges, unwaxed
    or well-scrubbed
1½ good and careless tablespoons
    sherry vinegar
40g pine nuts
good olive oil, to finish

Soak the sultanas in just-boiled water for an hour or so. Sprinkle the flour on to a plate and season with a generous pinch of salt and a couple of twists of black pepper. Heat 3 tablespoons of the oil in a large, heavy-based frying pan. The oil must be hot; otherwise by the time the fish is browned it will be overcooked. Roll the sardines in the flour, patting off any excess, and fry quickly in the oil until well browned on both sides and cooked. Remove to a serving plate, handling them carefully. Wipe the pan clean with a thick wad of kitchen paper.

Peel and halve the red onions and slice them as thinly as your patience will allow: the thinner, the better. Keep to one side. In a dry frying pan toast the cumin and coriander seeds until the coriander begins to pop; do not allow them to burn. Add 2 tablespoons oil to the pan, followed by the onions, drained sultanas, thyme sprigs and bay leaves, and fry gently. On no account allow the onions to colour; cook them until they are just beginning to soften. Season to taste.

Peel the rind from 1 of the oranges into wide strips and add to the pan. Squeeze the juice from both the oranges and pour over the onions. Add the sherry vinegar and bring to the boil. Cook until the liquid is reduced by a third. Remove from the heat and pour over the sardines in their dish. Cover and leave to stand for a minimum of 2 hours before serving, turning once.

Just before serving, put the pine nuts in a small, dry frying pan and cook for 5–6 minutes over a medium heat until golden brown, turning often so that they don't burn. Scatter the pine nuts over the sardines, dribble over some good olive oil and strew with some fresh young thyme leaves just before you bring the plate to the table. Eat with good bread for mopping up the juices and any onion or sultana stragglers.

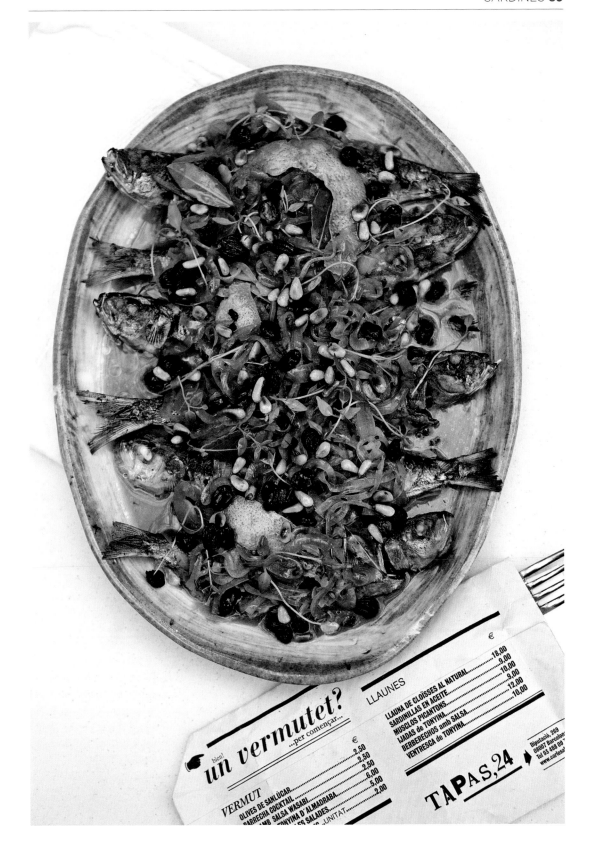

SEA BASS

The bass is a most handsome fish that I have chased along the South Coast from the Birling Gap to Weymouth Harbour and on to Boscastle. Whenever the opportunity has arisen, I have dedicated hours to this fish, armed with wriggling sand eels, gaudy plugs and an earful of local expertise/nonsense.

But despite all concentration and anticipation, things generally end in despondent journeys home. Only a scant handful of times have I gazed down, shaky-legged, at the prize lying on deck or shingle. So although I would love you to think that I have had many mighty battles with this silver sword, the sea bass is a fish I seem unable to get to grips with. I've lost all the decent ones and cursed every spider crab I thought was a take. Yet I seem to know that, one day soon, something good will happen.

In the kitchen sink, though, I have seen a fair few whoppers and am always amazed by their beauty and fascinated when finding the assortment of huge squid, crabs and mackerel inside them that show what swift and skilful hunters they are.

When handling bass, watch out for the dorsal spines; they hurt as if poison-tipped and it is most excruciating and unfortunate to get one in a finger. I have done this a couple of times and no more, I hope. Once, blubbing with a ghastly face and squeezing my throbbing red finger, it was a memorably painful episode, showing that this warrior fish seems to get the better of me, both in and out of its element.

Although farmed bass have become very cheap, wild line-caught bass are far superior in taste. In their firm white flesh, a pleasantly meaty taste is apparent. The resilient flesh is very versatile, responding well to the barbecue, and being excellent eaten raw in the Japanese style or as ceviche, the Latin American summer cooler. Steamed, roasted or fried, sea bass stands up well to strong tastes such as porcini, artichokes and charred asparagus. Wild bass is expensive, but you would see why if you tried it next to farmed. Stay away from wild bass if they look small; they are either not wild or, being that size, will never have bred.

BASS WITH CLAMS

I can't help but smile when looking at bass closely surrounded with piles of clams. Not only is it a dramatic and delicious dish, but it also reminds me of those trembling excited moments gazing down on a landed bass, with the clams closely resembling wet pebbles.

Serves 6

1 x 1.8kg line-caught sea bass, scaled,
    gutted and degilled
1 tablespoon flaked sea salt
ground black pepper
a good slug of olive oil, plus extra
    for oiling
1kg fresh live clams

125ml white wine
2 medium banana shallots
3 fat garlic cloves
1 tablespoon young thyme leaves
25g butter
a good pinch of saffron threads
1 unwaxed or well-scrubbed lemon
a handful of young curly
    parsley, chopped

Preheat the oven to 220°C/425°F/Gas 7. Trim the spiny fins from the bass with sharp scissors, taking heed to keep fingertips well away from the tips. Cut out and discard the gills if it hasn't already been done for you.

Securely cover an oven shelf with a double thickness of very well-oiled foil. Slash the fish 3 or 4 times deeply on each side and season all over heavily with salt and less so with black pepper. Pour a good slug of olive oil over the upturned side. Slide the shelf with the bass back into the oven. Bake in the centre of the oven for about 25 minutes. A knife inserted into the thick meat behind the fish's head should meet with only the faintest resistance at the point where you can imagine the tip is almost touching the bone.

While the bass is cooking, prepare the clams. Wash them well and discard any that don't close when tapped on the edge of the sink. Put them in a saucepan with the wine and place over a high heat. Cover and bring to the boil. Cook for 2–3 minutes at most, shaking the pan occasionally, until the clams have just steamed open. Don't be tempted to cook them longer, as they will be reheated later and should remain delicate in texture. Drain through a colander into a large bowl, reserving every last drop of their liquor. Set aside.

Peel and finely slice the shallots and garlic. Chop the thyme leaves very finely. Melt the butter in a medium saucepan over a low heat and gently fry the shallots, garlic and thyme until totally softened, but not coloured. Add the saffron, the juice of half the lemon and the reserved clam liquor. Bring to a simmer and cook until reduced by a third, stirring every now and then.

Go through the clams and throw away any selfish ones that haven't opened. When the bass is ready, put the clams in the pan with the saffron sauce. Warm through gently, shaking the pan every now and then until the clams are hot. Don't allow them to overcook or they will become rubbery.

Take the cooked fish out of the oven and slide gently on to a warmed serving platter. Spoon the clams and sauce around the fish and serve at once, all scattered about with parsley, and with the remaining lemon half, sliced. Don't forget to prize out the fish's succulent cheek meat.

Start by making the red sauce. Make a small cross in the base of each tomato with a sharp knife and cut out the green core. Put the tomatoes in a mixing bowl and cover with just-boiled water. Leave for about 30 seconds, then lift out with a slotted spoon. The skins should easily slip off. Cut the tomatoes into quarters and put them in a food processor. If they are whole, finely chop the chipotle chillies – you should end up with 2 good teaspoonfuls. Add this to the tomatoes along with the garlic cloves, oregano, cumin seeds, orange juice and sea salt. Blitz hard until all the ingredients are well blended and the sauce is almost smooth.

Heat a small frying pan and add the oil. When it is almost smoking, pour in the tomato and chipotle mixture and simmer furiously to reduce the liquid, evaporating most of the water out of the sauce. This should take 2–3 minutes. Shake the pan a few times to prevent the sauce from sticking. Remove from the heat and leave to cool.

To make the green sauce, cut the green tomatoes in half and put in a food processor. Peel the onion and roughly chop with the chile (seeds in). Wash the coriander to remove any dirt from the stalks and trim only the very ends. Put the leaves and stalks in the food processor with the tomatoes, onion, green chile, lime juice and salt. Blitz hard until the mixture is almost smooth – you may need to remove the lid and push the sauce down with a rubber spatula a couple of times until the right consistency is reached. Turn out the sauce into a small bowl and stir in the oil.

Place a large, flameproof griddle pan, frying pan or sturdy baking tray over a high heat (make sure that it will fit not only the fish but also completely under your grill before you use it). Preheat the grill to its hottest setting. Take the fish fillets and wipe dry with kitchen paper. Rub with a little sunflower oil and season generously with sea salt.

Put 1 of the fish fillets on a board, flesh-side uppermost, and spoon the red sauce generously all over, spreading to the sides with the back of the spoon. Lift carefully on to the griddle, skin-side down. Put the second fish fillet beside it, again skin-side down, and brush the flesh lightly with sunflower oil. Cook the fish for 4–5 minutes until the skin is very crisp.

Next, place the griddle under the grill, close to the heat source, and continue cooking for a further 4–5 minutes until the chipotle sauce begins to char in places. Remove from the heat, taking care because the griddle will be heavy and extremely hot. Lift the fillets on to a wooden board, placing them side by side. Spoon the green sauce over the bare fish fillet. Garnish with lime wedges and serve.

BASS WITH ROASTED RED PEPPERS

I make this often in the summer, preferably over a fire on my favourite beach in Dorset. I tend to eat the 2 parts together with nothing else but some good bread.

Serves 4–5

1 x 1.8kg line-caught sea bass, scaled,
    gutted and degilled
1 teaspoon olive oil
flaked sea salt

PEPPERS
4 large red peppers

6 anchovy fillets in olive oil, drained
4 new-season garlic cloves or 1 large
    good hard garlic clove
1 unwaxed or well-scrubbed lemon
1 heaped tablespoon baby capers, drained
3 tablespoons good extra virgin olive oil
flaked sea salt and ground black pepper
a handful of mint leaves (optional)
a handful of basil leaves (optional)

Put the peppers on a baking tray lined with foil and place under a preheated high grill for 10–12 minutes, turning occasionally, until the skin is totally blackened and blistered on all sides. Alternatively, lay them directly on the gas flame and char them this way, turning regularly. Don't shortcut this stage or the peppers will not be as tasty as they could be; they will look very burnt before peeling and this is right. Transfer to a bowl and cover with clingfilm or put in a lidded air-tight plastic container. Leave to stand for 10–15 minutes until cool enough to handle.

Turn the peppers on to a board and peel off the skin. On no account rinse the flesh under running water or you will lose the delicious flavour. Cut each pepper in half and allow the juice to run into a serving bowl. (If there is a lot of juice, reduce it in a small saucepan over a high heat until syrupy, then pour it into the serving bowl; this really intensifies the flavour.) Deseed the peppers and tear the flesh into long strips, about the width of your finger, into the serving bowl.

Finely chop the anchovies and peel and finely slice the garlic. Add both to the peppers. Peel 3 long strips from the lemon rind, twist, then drop them into the bowl. Squeeze over the juice from one half of the lemon and add the capers. Pour over the olive oil, add salt to taste and a couple of twists of black pepper, and toss well together. Leave to stand at room temperature for at least an hour to allow the flavours to get going.

Light the barbecue and leave it until the coals burn with a light dusting of pale grey ash covering their surface. First, wipe the bass clean of any wetness. This is important, as it will help prevent the fish from sticking on the grill. Rub it on both sides with the oil and season with plenty of salt.

Lay the bass over the coals on the hot grill rack and cook for about 15 minutes on each side until the skin is crisp and browned and the tip of a knife inserted into the thick meat behind the head meets with only the faintest resistance near the bone. Don't be tempted to prod the fish while it cooks. Turn it carefully so that it doesn't break. While the fish is cooking on the other side, roughly chop the mint and basil, and toss through the pepper salad. Slide the fish on to a board or platter, and serve with the peppers.

RED MULLET

RED MULLET WITH ROUILLE

This is kind of a fish soup – but without the soup, if that makes any sense.
Which it doesn't!

Serves 2

2 slices of fresh baguette
1 tablespoon olive oil
2 ripe beef tomatoes
1 tablespoon plain flour
flaked sea salt and ground black pepper
sunflower oil
2 red mullet fillets, scaled
lemon wedges, for squeezing over the fish
    (optional)

ROUILLE
a good pinch of saffron threads
2 large free-range egg yolks
6 anchovy fillets in olive oil, drained
3 tablespoons tomato ketchup
2 teaspoons harissa paste
juice of ½ lemon
3 large garlic cloves
100ml sunflower oil
50ml virgin olive oil

To make the rouille, first soften the saffron. Put the threads in a bowl and
only just cover with hot water. Leave for 10 minutes. Put the egg yolks,
anchovies, ketchup, harissa and lemon juice in a blender or food processor.
Add the saffron and its water with the peeled and roughly chopped garlic.
Blend together until well combined. With the motor running, slowly add both
the oils and blend until the rouille is smooth and glossy, taking the lid off a
couple of times to push the mixture down. It should not be too stiff, but
spread a little of its own accord when served. Preheat the grill to full blast.

    Cut 2 long diagonal slices from the baguette, brush with the olive oil and
toast under the grill. They should be nicely browned on both sides, but paler
in the middle and not brittle. Put these large croûtons on 2 plates. Thinly slice
the tomatoes. Sift the flour on to a plate and season with a good amount of sea
salt and a couple of twists of black pepper. Pour a little sunflower oil on to
another plate. Put a small frying pan over a high heat.

    Dip the fish fillets in the flour, coating lightly on just the skin side.
Pat off any excess. Now drag the fish through the oil, again skin-side down.
This ensures that you take only the amount of oil to the pan that you need.
Gently place the fillets skin-side down in the hot pan, where they should sizzle
instantly. Rest a small plate over them to keep them flat as they cook, and fry
for 4 minutes or until the skin is crisp and golden. Regulate the heat if it is
a little too fierce. Remove the plate. The fillets should still have a pinkness,
spanning about a finger's width, down the centre. Turn off the heat and flip
them over for 20 seconds.

Place the slices of tomato, slightly overlapping, over each large
croûton and season with salt and black pepper. Lift the fish from the pan and
place on top of the tomato. Dollop a generous spoonful of the rouille on the
centre of each fillet and eat while the fish is piping hot. A wedge of lemon can
be squeezed over if it is desired.

RED MULLET WITH BASIL AND POTATO PURÉE

This is based on a dish I was taught to cook at the Halcyon Hotel in London in those frantic kitchen days before I minded being shouted at. I love the pink and green together, and the taste is heaven.

Serves 4

2 tablespoons plain flour
flaked sea salt and ground black pepper
1 tablespoon sunflower oil
4 x 150g red mullet fillets, scaled

PURÉE
900g potatoes
150ml double cream
1 fat garlic clove, peeled and finely sliced
a very large bunch of fresh basil
100ml good olive oil
a splash of whole milk

First make the purée. Bring a large saucepan of salted water to the boil. Peel the potatoes and cut into large, even-sized chunks. Drop into the water and return to the boil. Reduce the heat slightly and simmer for about 20 minutes until totally soft to a poke with a knife. Pour the double cream into a small saucepan and add the garlic. Bring to a gentle simmer and cook for 10 minutes, stirring occasionally, until the garlic is softened. Put to one side.

Boil a kettle of water. Trim the basil leaves, discarding very tough stalks, and put in a bowl. Pour over the just-boiled water until covered and leave for 30 seconds. Drain in a sieve under running water until cold. Tip on to kitchen paper and pat dry. Transfer to a food processor, add the oil and blend until as smooth as possible. You may need to remove the lid and push the mixture down once or twice until a smooth consistency is reached. Drain the potatoes and wind them through the fine setting of a potato ricer with the garlic you have fished out of the cream. Otherwise mash the potatoes and garlic with a hand masher, eradicating as many lumps as possible. Add the cream and half the basil oil and whisk in. The mash should turn a pastel green. Return the potato to the pan with the milk to loosen it, and reheat gently for 2 minutes, stirring constantly. Check the seasoning. Keep warm.

Get a large frying pan very hot. Sift the flour on to a plate and add a good pinch of salt and 2 twists of black pepper. Pour the oil on to another plate. Dip the fillets in the flour, coating lightly just on the skin side. Pat off any excess. Drag the fish, skin-side down, through the oil. This ensures that you use only the amount of oil you need for frying. Gently place the fillets skin-side down in the hot pan, where they should instantly sizzle. Rest a plate over them to help keep them flat, and fry for 4 minutes or until the skin is crisp and golden. Regulate the heat if too fierce. Remove the plate. The fillets should have a finger's width of pinkness down the centre. Turn off the heat and flip them over for 20 seconds. Spoon the purée on to 4 warmed plates and place a fillet on top of each. Spoon over a little of any remaining basil oil. Serve at once.

PLAICE

CEVICHE

Ceviche works to no set rules, varying wildly in look and taste from Central to South America. I experienced one in Nicaragua that contained peas and pineapple. It was odd but good. Other firm, white fish, such as bass or bream, will do fine here, but I think the plaice works particularly well and it is very reasonably priced. It is imperative that the plaice be very fresh, as any trace of fishiness will spoil the end result.

Serves 6

3 ripe vine tomatoes
2 long green chillies or 1 small jalapeño
1 small red onion, peeled
a small bunch fresh coriander (20g)

1 orange
2 large juicy limes
flaked sea salt
2 teaspoons sunflower oil
1 x 900g whole plaice, gutted, filleted
   and skinned

Cut out the stalk of each tomato and slash a criss-cross in the skin at the bottom. Put in a bowl and cover with just-boiled water. Leave for no more than 30 seconds until the skins appear to split and wrinkle. Don't leave them for too long or the flesh will begin to cook in the hot water and turn to pap. Strip off the skin, using a small knife to lift any stubborn areas. Cut them into quarters from top to bottom and scoop out the seeds into a cup. Cut the flesh into small pieces and tip into a large bowl. Tip the seeds into a sieve and push through any juice into the chopped tomato. You want to maximize on juice.

Split the chillies lengthways and deseed. Dice them as finely as you can, keeping your fingers away from your eyes. Add to the tomatoes. I like a little violence from the chile, but alter the quantity as you wish. Dice the onion finely and rinse it in a sieve under cold water to lessen its intensity. Drain well and add to the tomato. Rinse the coriander of any soil and gently shake or flick away any excess water. Cut the stalks from the leaves and chop them very finely. Add to the bowl. Squeeze the orange and limes into the tomatoes. Add enough salt to balance the tartness. Stir in the sunflower oil.

Cut the fillets into bited-size chunks, slicing through them at an angle, and tip them into the marinade. Finely chop the coriander leaves and stir them through the dish. Cover and leave to stand in the fridge for 30 minutes. The fish should in effect 'cook' in the acid, turning from translucent to opaque. Do not keep overnight, as the fish will be over-'cooked'.

Spoon into small bowls and serve immediately with slices of salted avocado, plain tortilla chips (or in the Costa Rican style with salt crackers) and mayonnaise. Serve with a bottle of tequila that you plan to finish.

BREAM

BLACK BREAM VERACRUZ

Toes in sand, I first ate this on the Pacific side of Mexico. After endless glasses of cold beer mixed with lime juice and salt, and under scant protection from the sun, I had lost most of my pocket dollars at backgammon to a German tourist. Tipsy and secretly annoyed, this dish cheered me up no end. It is easy to prepare and also a good treatment for bass, huss and conger eel.

Serves 4

750g sea bream, scaled, gutted and degilled

SAUCE
1 large Spanish onion, peeled
a bunch of coriander, not too large
2 fat garlic cloves, peeled and thinly sliced
3 large, ripe vine tomatoes

3 tablespoons olive oil, plus more for the
    fish and to finish
1 fresh jalapeño chile or 2 tablespoons
    jarred jalapeños
10 green olives, pitted
juice of ½ lime
1 teaspoon capers, drained
flaked sea salt
20g flaked almonds

Preheat the oven to 200°C/400°F/Gas 6. Halve the onion lengthways and slice it into thin slivers. Cut the obvious stalk parts from the coriander and chop them very finely; put aside a good handful of the leaves to finish the dish. In a large saucepan sweat the onion with the garlic, chopped coriander stalks and olive oil over a low heat for 10 minutes. The onion should not colour.

While all this is going on, cut the stalks out of the tomatoes and criss-cross their bums. Put in a deep bowl and submerge in just-boiled water for 30 seconds. Skin and roughly chop them. Add them – flesh, seeds, juice and all – to the cooking onions. Without deseeding, thinly slice the jalapeño from nose to stalk and add to the pot. Slice the olives into little rounds and in they go. Squeeze in the lime juice and stir in the capers. Simmer with the lid off for 15 minutes. Season well with salt. Tip the almonds on to a baking tray and toast in the oven for 4–5 minutes until golden. Transfer to a plate and allow to cool.

Rinse the fish and pat it dry. Lay it on a board and give it 3 shallow slashes from head to tail on both sides, using a sharp knife angled away from its head. Rub all over with a bit of olive oil and salt both sides lightly. Transfer to a shallow ovenproof dish that accommodates head and tail. Spoon the sauce around it and cover the top tightly with foil. Bake in the preheated oven for 30–40 minutes. To check it is cooked, push the blade of a knife into the flesh just behind the top of the head. It should slide in easily with only the faintest resistance from the meat near the bone. Unwrap the foil. Dribble over a little olive oil, scatter with almonds and coriander leaves, and serve.

TUNA

POACHED TUNA WITH SALMORIGLIO

God, this is good – and so simple! It requires attention but not too much: minimal effort for a superb lunch. When choosing the tuna, make sure that it is not only very fresh, but also firm to the touch and a deep red, not brown.

Serves 4

1 medium fennel bulb, trimmed
1 small onion, peeled
1 long red chile
1 bulb of garlic
1 tablespoon fennel seeds
1 tablespoon coriander seeds
2 bay leaves
10 black peppercorns
600g very fresh, firm yellowfin tuna
    fillet, skinned and halved lengthways

1 unwaxed or well-scrubbed lemon
200ml olive oil
100ml white wine

SALMORIGLIO
a very very generous handful
    of marjoram
5 tablespoons extra virgin olive oil
juice of ½ small lemon
½ teaspoon flaked sea salt

Shave the fennel and onion on a mandoline or slice very finely. Cut the chile up to the stalk without separating the halves. Halve the garlic across the middle, leaving the skin on; you will use one half. Put half the onion and fennel with the fennel seeds, coriander seeds, bay leaves, chile and peppercorns in a small pan. Lay both halves of the divided tuna loin on top. All should fit snugly. Peel the lemon rind into wide strips and add with the rest of the fennel and onion, and the garlic half. Pour over the oil and wine. The fish should be submerged, but if it is not add more as needed, in the proportions 2 parts oil to 1 part wine. Bring to the boil over a high heat. As soon as the liquid is foaming, remove from the heat and leave to totally cool. (The tuna should be rare inside by the time the liquid comes to the boil and perfectly pink by the time it is cool enough to handle. This is why the tuna should fit snugly in the pan: too much space and liquid, and the tuna will be overcooked by the time the liquid has boiled.)

Meanwhile, make the salmoriglio. Pick the marjoram leaves from the stalks and chop very finely. Put in a small bowl and add the extra virgin olive oil, lemon juice (use the one peeled earlier) and sea salt. Stir and leave to stand.

When the liquid around the tuna can be handled, take out the fish and flake carefully. Where it is rare in the middle, gently prize the sheets apart with your thumb; don't tear at it. Lay the pieces about a plate and scatter with some fennel, onion, chile and lemon rind. Splash some juice about the fish and trail over the salmoriglio. This goes well with the French beans on page 167.

OCTOPUS

OCTOPUS IN THE SARDINIAN WAY

Octopus is one of the few meats improved by freezing. It can be rubbery when fresh, even when cooked with patience. Introducing it to a minus-zero temperature breaks down its obstinate cell structure, so I would advise freezing it before use if you know it is fresh – 48 hours should do the trick.

Susanah, a tiny, twinkling Italian matriarch who has fed me often and well, presented a happy table with this dish on one of my holidays to Sardinia. Among her other delights were such things as dogfish cooked with its liver pounded with capers and a deep-fried moray eel (that had previously tried to bite my toe off). If she read my interpretation of her recipe she would probably frown, shake her head, wag her finger and say sharply: 'No No No!'

Serves 4

8 medium octopus tentacles
1 bulb of garlic
50ml olive oil
12 salad onions or large spring onions,
    white part only, trimmed
juice of 1 lemon

2 fresh bay leaves
a big sprig of fresh thyme
8 black peppercorns
300g fresh peas (unpodded weight)
a generous knob of fridge-cold butter or
    a good slug of extra virgin olive oil
some wild fennel fronds (optional)

Defrost the octopus legs, if necessary, before cutting them up, at a slant, into big mouth-sized chunks. Leave the last 8cm at the tip of each tentacle in one piece, as they look great rolled up like the ringmaster's whip.

Chop the bulb of garlic horizontally through the middle and place both sides flesh-side-down in a heavy-based casserole into which you have poured the oil. Bring to a high heat until just before the oil begins to smoke. Throw in the onions and brown rapidly. At this point throw in the octopus; it should instantly sizzle, hiss and crackle loudly if the heat is correct. Push it around with a spoon. After 30 seconds, turn down the heat to very low. Squeeze in the lemon juice, add the bay leaves, thyme sprig and peppercorns, and cover with the lid.

After a couple of minutes, peek inside and you will see that the tentacle pieces are now swimming in a delicious purple-pink juice given up from the meat and in which they will now stew. Gently simmer it for 1 hour and 45 minutes on this very low heat. While the occy stews, shell all the peas into a bowl.

When the time is up, test the octopus for tenderness. A knife should slide into the flesh with ease. If not, give it another 15 minutes or so. Throw in the peas and cook with the lid off the pot, as this will allow the sauce to reduce while the peas cook. (If using frozen peas, make sure that they are first properly defrosted, as you don't want to introduce water back into the sauce you have been trying to reduce.)

After about 10 minutes, check the seasoning, then whisk in a generous knob of cold butter or alternatively pour over a good slug of extra virgin olive oil. Sprinkle over with loosely chopped wild fennel leaves if you happen to have the plant growing nearby.

Try to enjoy without looking over your shoulder for the giant tentacle of mother coming to wreak hell on those who took her little one…

CRAYFISH, PRAWNS & LANGOUSTINES

CRAYFISH TACOS

I have an ongoing war with the hordes of non-native signal crayfish in our rivers. Heavy casualties have been inflicted; the enemy is now thrown into disarray under a ferocious offensive of mayonnaise, hot butter and chile sauce. However, your help against the scuttling ranks is still needed.

The tortillas used for tacos in this country are considerably larger than many I have seen in Mexico. When using the corn or flour ones sold here, cut them down to the size of a small, round beer mat. This recipe makes the right amount for 2 standard Mexican servings, which come in threes. Ideally, the signal crayfish for this recipe should be fresh and alive. Packed in brine, their flesh becomes strangely withered and tasteless. If you cannot find crayfish, langoustines would work well as an alternative.

Serves 2

12 live signal crayfish or 6 langoustines
½ ripe avocado
6 small soft corn tortillas
6 teaspoons soured cream
sea salt
wedges of lime (optional)

CHILE SAUCE
1 large beef tomato
½ medium onion
½ teaspoon ground cumin
½ teaspoon dried oregano
a small handful of fresh coriander
juice of 1 lime
flaked sea salt
2 small chipotle chillies, deseeded
about 2 tablespoons sunflower oil
2 garlic cloves, peeled

Put a saucepan of water on to boil that is big enough for the crayfish. Cut the stalk base from the tomato and score the bottom with a criss-cross. Drop it in the boiling water for 30 seconds and remove to await later attention.

Bring the water back to the boil and drop in the crayfish. Cook them for no longer than 2 minutes. The same applies if you are using langoustines. Lift the shellfish out with a slotted spoon and plunge them into a large bowl of cold water to stop them cooking. Peel the little blighters, making sure you crack their claws, remove the black intestinal tracts, and lift out the sumptuous morsel of meat within. Discard the shells and put the meat to one side.

Skin the tomato, chop it in 4 and chuck it into a blender with the peeled and roughly diced onion. Add the cumin, oregano, stalks of the coriander (reserving the leaves), lime juice, ½ teaspoon salt and roughly chopped chillies. Hit go and whizz the lot into a smooth purée.

Get 1 tablespoon of the oil very hot in a frying pan over a high heat and pour in the tomato mixture, which should sizzle and spit the minute it hits the pan. Stir vigorously for about 3 minutes until it appears thickened and not watery. Remove the sauce from the pan and wipe it clean. Finely chop the garlic. Make a shallow cut down the curve of the peeled crayfish from neck to tail and poke out the waste sac with the tip of a small knife. Coarsely chop the meat. Prepare the avocado by peeling one half and slicing it lengthways into 6 slender pieces the width of a pencil. Pick a few whole leaves of the coriander.

Return the frying pan to a medium heat with ½ tablespoon oil and get it properly hot. Put another frying pan over a low heat on the next hob. Flick the garlic into the first frying pan and let it fry until just before it starts to change colour. Throw in the crayfish meat and stir it through the garlic. You should be hearing the joyous sound of sizzling at all times. Now add the tomato mixture, stirring all together until it is well heated. Add a tablespoon of water if it is getting too thick – but not too much: it should hold its shape and not leak water.

Dribble a couple of drops of oil into the other pan and use a tortilla to brush it around before joining it with 2 more tortillas. After 30 seconds or so the tortillas will soften as they warm. Turn them over to heat the other side. While still in the pan, put a spoonful of crayfish mix in each one. Lift them on to a plate and blob with a small dollop of soured cream. Top with a slice of the avocado, a small pinch of salt and a wee sprig of coriander. Serve to your compadre with a wedge of lime and a cold beer, or wolf them instantly and make some more. Repeat with the remaining tortillas. (*See* page 95 for tortilla suppliers.)

LANGOUSTINE RISOTTO

In my teens I frequented a restaurant called the Teatro di Pompeii on the Piazza Paradiso in Rome. Lino, the proprietor, was a most charming man, although he would not divulge the complete recipe to his techno-pink shrimp risotto. Its lurid colour was extraordinary and the taste pure essence of shrimp. Overall it remains a vivid memory.

I'm frustrated that in the UK it is next to impossible to buy uncooked Atlantic prawns, so I have replaced them with langoustines. As a result, this risotto is good, but sadly achieving the shocking pink is impossible.

Serves 4

12 raw Scottish langoustines, defrosted
    if frozen
2 small celery sticks
1 small onion
2 garlic cloves
25g butter
1 tablespoon olive oil
125ml dry vermouth, such as Noilly Pratt
a good pinch of saffron threads
200g risotto rice
50g butter, cut into cubes and chilled

a handful of finely chopped fresh
    chives, to finish
extra virgin olive oil, to finish

STOCK
all the shells, heads and claws of
    the langoustines
1 tablespoon olive oil
2 litres water
2 level tablespoons tomato purée
3 black peppercorns
1 teaspoon flaked sea salt

Hold each langoustine around the middle and dangle it upside down, gently splaying out the tail fins. Pinch the central one and gently twist while pulling. As it comes away you will see the waste sac coming with it. Pull it all the way out until released and discard. If this does not work with a few, don't worry. When shelled, just make a shallow cut the length of the back and hoick it out.

For the stock, break the heads and claws from the raw langoustines and peel the shell from the flesh. Roughly chop the flesh and put it in the fridge, covered, until later. Heat the olive oil in a saucepan and allow it to get very hot before throwing in all the heads, shells and claws. Fry them hard for 4 minutes or so, then use a rolling pin or sturdy mug to smash and pound them with vigour, really taking care to crush out the juices from the heads. Fill the pan with the water and add the tomato purée and peppercorns. Bring the stock to a gently rolling simmer and cook for 45 minutes, after which you would be hard pushed to extract any more flavour from the shells. Add the salt.

In the meantime, de-string, wash and finely chop the celery. Peel and finely chop the onion and garlic. Soften these (the *soffritto*) gently in the 25g butter and the olive oil in a wide heavy-based saucepan over a medium heat (do not brown), then add the vermouth. Cook until evaporated. Turn off the heat.

When the stock is done, strain it through a sieve and measure 1.4 litres.

Pour this into a saucepan, add the saffron and return it to the heat. Bring it to the boil, then turn it down to a simmer. It is important that the stock is boiling; when it is added to the rice, the whole cooking process should be kept going at a high temperature rather than the rice soaking in lukewarm stock.

Bring the celery, garlic and onion *soffritto* back up to heat and tip in the dry rice. Fry it gently for 2 minutes, stirring constantly. Add the first ladleful of stock. It should bubble furiously, so don't get the tip of your nose steamed off. The idea now is to treat the risotto like a demanding baby. Feed it only when absolutely necessary – and this demands constant attention. When all the liquid has gone, add another ladleful and stir the rice, making sure that it is not catching on the bottom. Adjust the heat to a healthy but non-violent bubbling. Feed and occasionally stir for about 20 minutes. When it is done, the rice grains will have tripled in size and should be plump and soft but neither mushy (overcooked) nor chalky in the centre (undercooked). Test the rice every now and then. It should be creamy but not totally loose and certainly not clumpy. Ideally, it will migrate a little on the plate but not be splashy. If the stock is good, it will have left an unmistakable langoustine flavour as it evaporated during cooking. Two minutes before the end of the cooking time, stir in the langoustine flesh. Check the salt seasoning.

Turn off the heat and add the remaining fridge-cold butter. It must be cold to become creamy in the rice. Stir it through and cover with a lid. Allow to stand for 5 minutes or so while you herd everyone to the table. Spoon on to plates and scatter over some finely chopped chives with a splash of good extra virgin olive oil. Resist the temptation to aerially bombard with Parmesan.

NOTE: This works well with 1 large handful of chopped wild garlic leaves stirred in for the last 5 minutes of cooking.

PRAWN TANGIERS

This dish was plonked gruffly before me on a table in a dark and lurky harbourside establishment. Surrounded by hostile-looking Moroccan pirates, I really did not expect to eat one of the most delicious dishes of my life. I've christened it after the town of its origin.

Serves 2

100g fresh uncooked prawns
2 large-handed grabs of large
    spinach leaves
2 fat vine tomatoes

1 garlic clove
1 level teaspoon cumin seeds
3 tablespoons olive oil
juice of ¼ small lemon
flaked sea salt and ground black pepper

You will need 1 small frying pan. I would also note that adult spinach is preferable here, not only for its stronger taste, but also because the same amount of baby spinach will fry away to weedy patheticness.

Get each prawn ready by peeling the shell away. Make an incision down the back and hoick out the black intestine and discard. Roughly chop the prawns and put to one side.

Wash the spinach free of beasties, by all means life-guarding any that appear to be poor swimmers. If the stalks are particularly fibrous, snap them off and discard. Bunch up the spinach and chop it roughly. Cut the stalk base from each tomato, criss-cross the other end and cover in just-boiled water for 30 seconds. Tip away the water and peel off the skins. Chop the tomatoes roughly, but not too large, taking care to save the seeds and juice. Peel and finely chop the garlic.

Take the frying pan and dry-fry the cumin seeds over a medium heat until their aroma comes to the nose, by which time they will be nicely toasted. Now add 2 tablespoons of the olive oil, followed quickly by the spinach. It will crackle and pop as you add it. Turn in the pan, adding fresh leaves as you go until it is all in and wilted. Now add the tomatoes, garlic, lemon juice and a good amount of salt and black pepper. Cook together fairly rapidly, stirring occasionally, making sure that the contents don't stick and burn. You want to get rid of an obviously watery appearance without drying out the dish. Transfer to a bowl and, without washing out the pan, add the remaining oil, then return the pan to a medium-high heat.

Fry the roughly chopped prawn meat briskly until opaque and a little golden (a couple of minutes or so). Flop the spinach and tomato mixture back on top. Cook until bubbling and serve immediately in the Moroccan style with warm white rolls and mint tea (*see* page 265).

LOBSTER

I once heard a farcical story of 2 girls left to boil a couple of gigantic blue lobsters while their men friends left the house on an armed ramble.

The dizzy cooks thought it sensible to remove the yellow rubber bands from their Goliath claws and plopped the apparently drowsy creatures into the rolling water. They had unwittingly unleashed a terrifying scene unparalleled by any story from distant oceans.

The enraged, scalded and half-red lobsters levered themselves from the upturned pot, with the kitchen now resembling a Turkish bath. Through the swirling steam flashed their crimson claws, slashing wildly in revenge and confusion. The sound of their fearsome snipping was said to be deafening.

Fearing for their elegant ankles, the girls took to higher ground in the form of 2 rickety stools. After the hot mist had cleared, the lobsters showed no signs of forgiveness. However, it appeared obvious that they had been confused in the fiasco, as they were now demolishing a third stool on the other side of the kitchen.

Leaping from her stool, bold Fran flew, hand outstretched, to grab a stiff-bristled broom leaning nearby. In a moment of unrivalled bravery, and with a hair-raising war cry, she swept Neptune's guard lobsters, in one run, out of the back door on to the patchy grass.

The men, returning to this dreadful scene, immediately reacted in a wasteful and misplaced moment of St George-ishness. Having shot the tormented creatures, the garden was wrecked with 4 smoking craters.

Idiots! This is no end for such a noble animal. I love lobsters and feel an understanding of them. They are worriers and I empathise with their grumpy but harmless nature. I'd prefer you to kill them swiftly, so either dispatch them with a fine skewer run into the small indent on top that is midway down the head, or pop them into the freezer for 15 minutes before boiling.

LOBSTER MOJO DE AJO

This involves you killing the lobster with a knife. It's actually a quick and humane way to dispatch them, if unsuitable for those who refer to deer as 'Bambi' or buy cards with misty kittens on the front. Perfect for the barbecue, this recipe transports me back to happy holidays spent in swimming trunks, sitting on the beer cooler and tossing shells into the sea.

Serves 2–4

1 x 900g live lobster

MOJO DE AJO SAUCE
1 generous bulb of garlic
roughly 125ml light olive oil

2 plump chipotle chillies, deseeded and
  finely chopped
juice of 1 large lime
flaked sea salt
coriander leaves, to garnish
lime wedges, to serve

To make the mojo de ajo sauce, first peel all the garlic cloves and chop to medium-fine. Put in a small saucepan and cover with light olive oil. Bring the oil up to the gentlest simmer, allowing the little lemonade lines of tiny bubbles to rise from the garlic. Do not allow it to overheat or boil at any cost or the garlic will burn. Scientific attention is needed. The garlic is ready when it begins to turn an old ivory colour. This will take 10–15 minutes. At this point drop in the finely chopped chipotles, the lime juice and ½ teaspoon salt. After 30 seconds, turn off the heat and allow the mixture to stand for at least 3 hours. The recipe need hardly continue. Forget the lobster and eat the sauce with warm crusty bread. It's delicious.

When ready to cook the lobster, light the barbecue and leave to burn until a light dusting of grey ash covers the coals.

Do not remove the bands from the lobster's claws until you have killed it, as this will only result in severed fingers on the kitchen floor, high-pitched screams and a furious, rattled lobster. Go about killing your dinner with swift respect. Squeamish scrapings on the shell with a knife will only distress the lobster. Lay the lobster flat on a board and hold it down firmly with a cloth to prevent it arching up. Deftly and without hesitation drive the point of a large, heavy knife into the middle of its head where the cross is and down through to the board. Lever the blade down to cut between the eyes. Turn the lobster around. Put the blade back into where you made the first entry and cut the other way straight down and through the middle of the tail section. (Any subsequent movement is purely nerves and I assure you the lobster is dead.)

Remove the green parts inside the lobster's head and throw away with the snipped-off elastic bands. Use a rolling pin to crack the claws – without pulverising them – and leave the shell on. Brush the tail meat generously with the garlic oil, but not the delicious sediment in the bottom. Salt lightly.

Put the lobster on the barbecue, flesh-side down. Cook for 4 minutes before turning on to the shell side and cooking until it has all turned vibrant red. (You can also cook the lobster under the grill for 5 minutes on each side.) Lift off the rack and put on a serving plate. Spoon over the sauce liberally, ensuring that you get lots of garlic and chile from the bottom. Garnish the empty head cavity with coriander leaves and put lime wedges on the top for squeezing. Serve with cold beer.

LOBSTER WITH MELON AND CURRIED MAYONNAISE

This recipe may suggest I eat so much lobster that I'm bored and make weird things like this with it. Not so! I just don't necessarily want it grilled all the time. Certainly, this is a little naff in presentation, maybe outdated – very eighties, indeed – but it's good, so who cares?

When choosing the melon, it must be ripe or it will really let the side down. A good way to tell is to smell the melon, and if it doesn't smell of itself (and by that I mean that it smells of nothing), it's not ready for you.

Serves 3

1 tablespoon flaked sea salt
4 black peppercorns
1 x 700g live lobster, chilled in the freezer
    for 15 minutes
½ ripe cantaloupe or other small variety
    of honeydew melon
a few fresh chives, tarragon leaves
    or both

MAYONNAISE
2 large free-range eggs
4 teaspoons Dijon mustard
2 capfuls of tarragon vinegar
1½ level teaspoons mild curry powder
50ml olive oil
100ml sunflower oil
a squeeze of lime juice
flaked sea salt

Bring a saucepan of water, big enough to just submerge the lobster, to the boil. Add the salt and peppercorns. Lower the lobster in swiftly. Do not remove the rubber bands from the claws when the lobster is alive unless you are excited by danger. As soon as the water returns to the boil, turn off the heat and leave it there for 12 minutes. After this time, remove the lobster and allow it to cool. Discard the water except for a cup's worth.

Plop the egg yolks for the mayonnaise in a high-sided bowl with the mustard, vinegar and curry powder. Whizz with a stick blender while slowly dribbling the oils in together. If the mayonnaise gets a little stiff, splash in a small amount of the lobster water to let it down and finish pouring in the oil. The mayo should hold its own but not be rigid. Get the acidity to your liking with the lime juice, remembering that it should not be too tart, just very mildly tangy. Season with salt to taste.

Break away the lobster's tail from the head and peel away the shell. Crack the claws and their arm sections and carefully tease out all the meat. Placing the tail on the board, halve it lengthways, then slice it in morsels the width of 2 x £1 coins. Roughly chop the claw meat. In a mixing bowl, combine the lobster and enough mayonnaise so that it is not smothered but instead rather nicely coated. Chill for half an hour, covered.

When you are ready to eat, scoop the seeds out of the melon half

EGGS, YOGHURT & CHEESE

EGGS

ASPARAGUS AND SORREL OMELETTE

The omelette is a great, and somehow a manly, thing. Then again, this is waffle. If sorrel is hard to find, make it without.

Serves 1

6 fairly thin asparagus spears
3 large free-range eggs, at room
    temperature
a dash of single cream

flaked sea salt and ground black pepper
a small knob of butter
a dash of sunflower oil
a good handful of sorrel leaves,
    washed and shredded
finely snipped chives, to serve

Trim the asparagus, removing any tough ends from the stalks (these can be kept for soups). Plunge into a large pan of boiling water. Return to the boil and cook for 3–4 minutes until totally tender. Tip immediately into a colander and rinse under running water until cold. Drain well. Slice the spears into short, diagonal strips.

Whisk the eggs thoroughly with the cream and plenty of salt and black pepper. In a small, non-stick frying pan, preferably with curved sides, melt the butter with the oil over a medium heat until smoking.

Pour in the egg mixture and scatter over the blanched asparagus and the shredded sorrel leaves. Cook for 10 seconds or so before lifting the pan just above the heat and jerking it back towards you in a circular motion with the pan slightly angled downwards. Keep the mixture moving all the time. This will start to roll the omelette into a cocoon shape. Alternatively, you can fold the omelette over after a minute or so using a spatula, but in this case it needs to be cooked over a lower heat in order not to burn. Cook for 5–6 minutes to the point where it no longer weeps runny egg. This should still give you a nice gooey centre.

Gently roll the omelette on to a plate, scatter it with chopped chives and descend on it.

CHEESE

FRUITALIA

The name of this recipe has become a bit of a joke for me as, on asking random Turkish people about it, they look nonplussed and walk away briskly. I am now convinced that since my Turkish holiday 12 years ago I have remembered something wrong. Whatever the name, the recipe requires a small frying pan, as it is important that the eggy cake and filling remain deep in the same way as a Spanish tortilla.

Serves 2

3 big handfuls small broad beans
    (unpodded amount)
1 small red onion, peeled
2 tablespoons olive oil

flaked sea salt
6 large free-range eggs
ground black pepper
100g feta cheese
a small bunch of fresh mint

Pod the broad beans (you'll need about 200g podded weight) and cook them in a saucepan of boiling water for 3 minutes. Cool under cold water, drain and peel them from their shells. Roughly chop the onion. In a small frying pan, sauté the onion in the olive oil with a pinch of salt until totally softened but not coloured. Preheat the grill to full blast.

While the onion cooks, whisk the eggs well in a bowl with a little more salt and a good grind of black pepper. Really try to get as much air into them as you can.

When the onions are done, turn up the heat to medium and pour in the egg mixture; it should bubble away. Crumble in the feta and tear in the mint leaves, in small pieces. Scatter in the broad beans. Regulate the heat if needs be; over the next 2 minutes the eggs should colour and brown, but they should not burn.

Lift the pan off the heat and place under the grill for another 2–3 minutes. Cook until firm on the top when pressed and pleasantly squidgy in the middle but not wobbly. Place a suitable plate upside down over the pan, then upend it, so turning the fruitalia out on to the plate. Eat with crusty white bread. Despite not knowing the name, it is delicious!

RICOTTA AND HERB RAVIOLI

This is most delicate while at the same time heady with herbs. I love making ravioli; it's a meditation and the pale pasta and oil are truly beautiful in the warm rays of the sun at lunchtime.

Serves 4

3 large free-range eggs, plus 6 egg yolks
500g '00' pasta flour or a mixture of pasta
   flour and very fine semolina
2–3 tablespoons very fine semolina,
   extra for dusting
1 teaspoon flaked sea salt
ground black pepper
Parmesan cheese, for grating at the end

RICOTTA AND HERB FILLING
2 handfuls of pine nuts (about 75g)
450g good-quality ricotta cheese

75g finely grated fresh Parmesan cheese
   (not the stuff in tubs)
3 tablespoons finely chopped fresh
   marjoram leaves
1 tablespoon finely chopped fresh
   mint leaves
2 tablespoons finely chopped fresh
   basil leaves
finely grated rind of ½ unwaxed or
   well-scrubbed lemon
flaked sea salt and ground black pepper

GARLIC OIL
6 new-season garlic cloves (3 if older)
4–5 tablespoons extra virgin olive oil

To make the pasta, beat the eggs and egg yolks in a jug. (This is so that when put in the food processor the egg yolks won't streak the dough.) Put the flour in a food processor. With the motor running, slowly add the eggs. Mix until the dough forms a ball. If it appears too dry, add a few drops of water. It should not be tacky – more like children's playdough. Wrap the pasta in clingfilm and allow it to chill for an hour or so.

Tip the dough on to a board scattered liberally with very fine semolina and knead the dough by pushing it away with the heel of your hand, then folding it back towards you. Twist a quarter turn and repeat. You'll need to do this for about a minute, or until it is smooth with a slight sheen. Cover with clingfilm and leave to rest in the fridge for 1 hour.

To make the filling, first toast the pine nuts in a dry frying pan over a low heat until golden brown. Move them continually so that they do not burn. Tip them into a mixing bowl. Put the ricotta and grated Parmesan in with the pine nuts. Add the herbs to the mix with the finely grated lemon rind. Season carefully with salt, as the Parmesan will have, to a degree, seasoned the mix already, and well with the black pepper. Mix well. Cover and put to one side until needed.

To make the garlic oil, peel the garlic and cut into paper-fine slices from end to end. Pour the olive oil in a pan and get it warm. Turn off the heat and drop in the garlic, swirl it around and put to one side. It is important to cut the garlic thinly, as it will be eaten virtually raw.

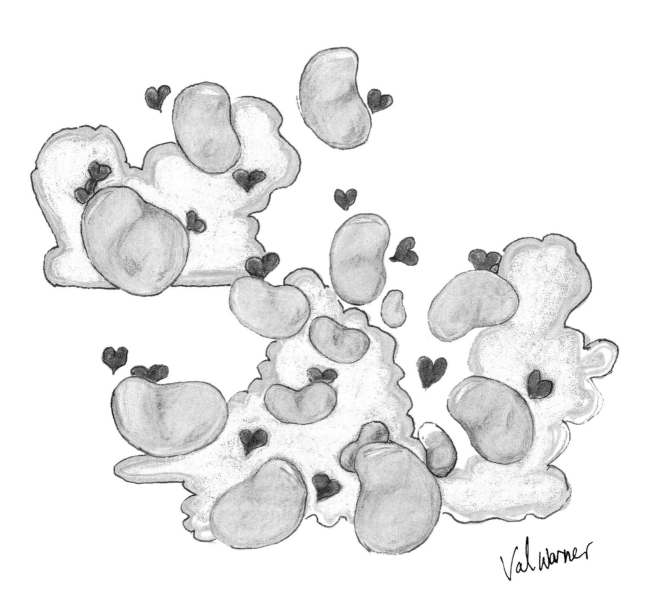

Val Warner

LEAF, STEM & ROOT

ASPARAGUS

ASPARAGUS WITH HOLLANDAISE SAUCE

Melted butter, great! Vinaigrette, fine! But hollandaise – oh God, what a combination! There is no better luxury to bring to the mouth on the end of a quivering green spear. Don't get me wrong, I do adore asparagus. I'm bad-mannered and greedy for it, but sometimes it's just a vehicle for hollandaise.

Serves 4

500g asparagus spears

HOLLANDAISE SAUCE
75ml white wine vinegar
juice of ½ lemon
225g unsalted butter, diced
3 large free-range egg yolks
flaked sea salt and ground black pepper

You can be sure you take only the tender part of the asparagus to the pot by bending it from end to end until it snaps and keeping the spear, but I think this wasteful. I like to chew on the fibrous, gnarly part at the table and get what I can. However, if you do want only the tender part, save the bases, as they make great soup.

Wash the asparagus, then make the hollandaise. Put the vinegar and lemon juice in a saucepan and bring to the boil. Leave to bubble furiously until it is reduced to around 2 tablespoons of liquid, then transfer to a largeish bowl. Leave to cool for a few minutes. Put the butter in another saucepan and heat gently until melted. As it bubbles, skim away the little white islands of milk solids that rise to the top. Don't cook it over too high a heat or it will burn. Carefully pour the hot clarified butter through a fine sieve into a warmed jug and discard any white, milky sediment left behind.

Half-fill a saucepan with water and bring to a simmer. Beat the egg yolks into the vinegar reduction and place the bowl so that it perches on top of the pan without touching the water. Beat with an electric whisk, or furiously with a hand one, until thick and very pale. Gradually add the melted butter to the egg yolks in a dribbly stream, whisking constantly until the sauce is thick and glossy. Remove the pan from the heat to prevent the sauce from overheating, and season with salt and a couple of twists of black pepper. Cover the surface with a sheet of clingfilm to stop a skin forming and put to one side in a warmish place while the asparagus is cooked.

Add the asparagus to the water and cook until just tender (this takes 3–5 minutes, depending on the thickness of the spears). Drain well and pile on to a warmed serving plate. Spoon the hollandaise sauce into a small dish and serve with the hot asparagus.

ASPARAGUS A LA OUTDATED

However old-fashioned, I love this kind of thing. It reminds me of Mum, a truly wonderful cook, who used to make her own version of it every now and then. It may seem perverse to buy fresh asparagus only to make it taste like it is tinned, but I think this is an achievement. Tinned asparagus has a great taste, as many seventies diners will vouch.

Serves 8

1 medium onion
25g butter
1 tablespoon sunflower oil, plus extra for
    oiling the mould
1.5kg asparagus spears
2 heaped teaspoons medium curry powder
150ml cold water

6 sheets of gelatine (approx. 20g)
4 large free-range egg yolks
juice of ½ lemon
1 teaspoon celery salt, plus sea salt to taste
75ml olive oil
100ml sunflower oil
125ml single cream
finely chopped fresh chives, to serve
white Melba toasts, to serve

Peel and finely chop the onion. Melt the butter with the oil in a large frying pan and fry the onion over a medium heat for 2–3 minutes until it is beginning to soften.

Meanwhile, wash and then finely slice the asparagus spears. Tip the slices into the pan with the onion and cook over a low heat for 5 minutes, stirring occasionally. Sprinkle the curry powder over and fry for a minute or so. Add the cold water and cover the pan loosely with a lid. Cook for 45 minutes, stirring occasionally, until the asparagus is very soft. Add a little more water if the pan appears dry at any time, but don't swamp the vegetables. Remove from the heat and leave to cool for 30 minutes.

Tip the asparagus mixture into a food processor and blend until as smooth as possible – you may need to remove the lid and push the mixture down a couple of times with a rubber spatula. Submerge the gelatine sheets in a bowl of cold water and leave for 5 minutes to soften.

Press the asparagus mixture through a fine sieve with the back of a ladle. Really work it so as to make as much purée as possible, then return the purée to the food processor. Discard what's left in the sieve. Add the egg yolks, lemon juice, celery salt and sea salt to taste. Blend until well combined, then, with the motor running, gradually add the oils in a thin trickle and continue blending until the mixture looks glossy and creamy, like a wet mayonnaise. Season with a little more celery salt if needs be and some finely ground white pepper.

Pour the cream into a small saucepan and heat gently until warm, but do not allow to simmer. Drain the gelatine and squeeze out the excess water. Drop the gelatine into the warm cream and stir vigorously until dissolved. Leave to cool until just tepid, then slowly add to the asparagus mixture and blend for a few seconds.

Pour the asparagus cream into a lightly oiled metal ring mould or bowl (1.2 litres in capacity). Cover with clingfilm and chill for 6–8 hours, or overnight, until set.

When ready to serve, turn out the mould by upending it on to a plate. Sometimes it needs no assistance, but if it is obstinate dip the mould in hot water for a few seconds. This should release the side. Scatter with some finely chopped chives and serve with white Melba toasts. Do not dish up too much per person, as it is very rich. It goes well with half a cold, peeled soft-boiled egg.

COURGETTE

DEEP-FRIED COURGETTE FLOWERS

These little crispy sceptres of ultimate pleasure will knock you sideways with their crunchy batter, hot anchovy cheese and delicate courgetteness. But watch out! In your rush to bite them you may blister your lip and burn your fingers and be caught in a precarious kitchen jig of pain and cheese, the 2 scalded areas joined with long, melty bubblegum strands of mozzarella.

Makes 6

6 baby courgettes with flowers
sunflower oil, for deep-frying
3 tablespoons strong white flour
flaked sea salt and ground black pepper
lemon wedges, for squeezing

FILLING
75g buffalo mozzarella, drained

3 good-quality anchovy fillets in
    olive oil, drained
flaked sea salt and ground black pepper

BATTER
75g strong white flour
½ teaspoon bicarbonate of soda
2 tablespoons lightly beaten
    free-range egg
a good pinch of flaked sea salt
125ml chilled fizzy water or light lager

To prepare the filling, cut the mozzarella into 12 short lengths, roughly 2.5cm long and 1cm wide. Place on a pile of kitchen paper and press gently to remove as much excess liquid as possible. If this isn't done, the batter around the flower head will become soggy, leach water when they are cut and spoil what should be a crispy and glorious experience.

Transfer the mozzarella to a board lined with more kitchen paper. Cut the anchovies in half lengthways and wrap a sliver around each rectangle of mozzarella. Season with black pepper and a pinch of salt.

Taking 1 courgette at a time, unfurl the delicate flower, being careful not to tear it. Open it up in the palm of your hand and poke 1 piece of the mozzarella and anchovy inside it with the sensitivity of a doctor investigating earache. Twist the petals around the filling to enclose snugly and repeat with the remaining courgettes and filling.

To make the batter, sift the flour and bicarbonate of soda into a large bowl and add the egg and a pinch of salt. Gradually add the lager, mixing briefly with a large whisk to get a light batter the consistency of a thick milkshake. Do not overwhisk, as you will bash all the bubbles out and when fried it will be toughened and un-airy.

Half-fill a large saucepan with sunflower oil. Put on the hob and heat to 180°C/350°F. Sift the flour into a shallow dish and season well with some salt and black pepper. When the oil is hot enough, take a courgette and turn it in the seasoned flour. Hold the floured courgette at each end and roll it in the batter so that it is evenly covered. Carefully drop it into the hot oil.

Follow the same method with a second courgette and cook both at the same time for about 2½ minutes or until crisp and golden brown, turning with metal tongs after the first minute. Do your manoeuvring work with care so as not to break the crispy armour and flood the flower with oil. Sometimes the courgettes are a little reluctant, annoyingly bobbing back again, but persevere as they need to cook on both sides. Keep an eye on the temperature of the oil – using a thermometer – and watch out for splashes.

When the batter is suitably crisp and deep golden brown, lift the courgette out of the hot oil with tongs and drain on plenty of kitchen paper. They can be put in a warm oven briefly while the others cook. Lift out any crisp pieces of batter from the oil with a slotted spoon and crunch on them while you continue preparing the remaining courgettes.

Serve the deep-fried courgette flowers immediately with a squeeze of lemon and a sprinkling of sea salt or, even better, dressed with the salmoriglio on page 111.

BABY COURGETTES AND CHANTERELLES WITH BASIL

This is simple harmony, coupled with the feeling of joy at how little is required to produce something so modest and utterly pleasing. I always eat this alone, so write it for one.

Serves 1

1 large grabbing-handful of chanterelles
5 baby courgettes
3 tablespoons olive oil

a generous pinch of flaked sea salt
1 garlic clove
ground black pepper
juice of ¼ lemon
a small handful of fresh basil leaves

Clean the chanterelles with a small knife and damp tea-towel, removing the stalk bases, moss and other dirt. Leave the small ones whole and tear the larger ones down the middle. Drop them into a mixing bowl.

Don't bother to remove the courgette stalks, as they are still tender; just trim the ends. Rinse the courgettes before slicing them lengthways into 3 or 4 long strips. Put them in the bowl with the mushrooms, dribble over 2 tablespoons of the olive oil and scatter with the salt. Tumble around together until all is thoroughly oiled.

Put a frying pan on the heat and get it fiercely hot so that the chanterelles and courgettes crackle and spit instantly. It should be a big pan so that everything is not crammed together. Throw in the contents of the mixing bowl. Resist the temptation to poke around all the time. At first water will weep out as the ingredients wilt, but when this has evaporated they will begin to colour quickly and this is the time to shake them around a bit.

Cook everything until well coloured and even a little burnt. This will take 7–8 minutes. Peel and finely chop the garlic. Turn off the heat and throw in the garlic. Add a good grind of black pepper and check if the dish still needs a smidgen more salt. Transfer to a soup plate. Pour over the remaining olive oil and squeeze over the lemon juice. Drop on the basil, roughly torn, and eat immediately with a good glass of chilled wine. Yippee!

TOMATOES

When asked what is my favourite fruit, I usually say peach. But come to think of it, I ought to say tomato because that is what it is – a fruit. And here I would quickly like to point out something else I find intriguing. Being a member of the Nightshade family, the tomato is a close cousin of the potato, chile and aubergine, as their pretty flowers will show you.

A good hothouse tomato has to have one of the greatest smells on earth. I would love to be able to describe it, but I cannot. As for their feel, well, a ripe tomato is a sexy thing just dying to be squeezed, and when the fingers go in, the fruit squidges out and juice runs down your arm … enough!

On the table, tomatoes hardly need help and when combined with bread, salt or oil they need little more interference. Some of my most memorable times in the field and abroad have invariably featured a good view, a great tomato, salt and a penknife. Splendid fat beef tomatoes, covered in onions and oil, draw me to the summer table just as fresh red sauces armed with chile leave me impatient for the spaghetti to boil. They make a fine start to the day, as many Spaniards will agree, and grilled on toast, with butter galore, a better TV companion would be hard to find.

Then, as winter sets in, I eat them only as tinned soup and ketchup, and struggle on with defining the smell of the hothouse tomato.

PAN CON TOMATO

This has recently become my favourite breakfast, usually made for me by my girlfriend Charlotte, who serves it up with strong sweet coffee. It is essential that the tomatoes be excellent and juicy. This is the Andalucian version of the dish, which excludes the garlic.

Serves 2

2 medium ripe tomatoes

flaked sea salt and ground black pepper
extra virgin olive oil
toasted sliced white bread, to serve

Cut the tomatoes into rough pieces and put in a bowl. Season with a very big pinch of flaked sea salt and a couple of twists of black pepper. Add a generous slug of your best olive oil. Blitz using a stick blender or liquidiser until as smooth as possible. Spoon and spread over of hot slices of lightly toasted baguette or Spanish rustic loaf that you have stabbed a few times with a fork and serve immediately with mugs of steaming coffee and a good newspaper. Marvel at how simple and delicious a breakfast can be.

SPAGHETTI ARRABIATA

This is one of my favourite pasta dishes. I think onion has no place in the sauce and, on asking a Roman friend for confirmation, he stamped a fist on the table followed with 'Never!'. I cannot argue the Parmesan, but I like just the tomato sauce, pasta and a little olive oil with no other interference. The growly faint back-of-throat chile burn is the point.

Serves 2

425g ripe tomatoes
1 hot red chile
3 tablespoons olive oil
4 garlic cloves, peeled and finely chopped

a squirt of lemon juice
½ teaspoon flaked sea salt
½ teaspoon caster sugar
170–200g dried spaghetti
extra virgin olive oil, to serve

Cut a small cross in the bum of each tomato, cut out the stalk bases, then cover with boiling water. Leave for 30 seconds, then pour away the water. Peel the tomatoes, cut them into quarters and scoop out the seeds into a small bowl. Chop the flesh roughly but small (so when cooked it has a puréed texture).

Deseed the chile and chop it finely. Heat the oil in a medium saucepan and throw in the chile. It should sizzle for a minute until it noticeably lightens in colour. Add the garlic and fry for no more than 30 seconds before adding the tomato flesh. They should also spit and sizzle on entry. Add the lemon juice (just enough to give it a faint edge), salt and sugar, then turn down the heat. Chuck the seeds.

Push the juice from the tomato seeds through a sieve into the pan. Simmer the sauce briskly for about 15–20 minutes, or until it starts going 'plup, plup, plup', slightly spattering the surrounding hob. You want the visibly watery element to have left the sauce. Check the seasoning.

Cook the pasta according to the packet instructions and drain it well. Add the pasta to the sauce and mix. Transfer the pasta to 2 plates and splash with excellent olive oil. I like to eat it leaning against the kitchen top.

TOMATO AND ONION SALAD

This is such a great salad, but it is imperative that the tomatoes be excellent or the exercise is pointless. I love large beef tomatoes, but good vine tomatoes are excellent too. I suggest that this is made just before eating.

Serves 2

4 beef tomatoes
flaked sea salt and ground black pepper

1 small red onion
4–5 tablespoons olive oil
red wine vinegar (optional)
fresh basil leaves (optional)

Wash and dry the tomatoes, then cut out the stalks. Put each tomato on its side and, with a large, sharp knife, slice it to the width of 2 x £1 coins. Lay the slices out flat and slightly overlapping, spiralling them out to the edge of a large plate from the centre. Scatter generously with salt and plenty of pepper.

Peel the red onion and slice it very finely into rings. Separate the rings a little before scattering them over the tomatoes. Splash liberally with the olive oil. Sometimes I also like to splash about a little red wine vinegar, with a thumb placed over the bottle opening. Add torn basil, should you want it.

This salad is very good if the onion is replaced with a few cloves of excellent and finely sliced garlic, and spring onions go well too.

PICNIC CRUDITÉ LOAF

I cannot remember where I saw this dish first, but I do recall a sixties-looking book with a sun-bleached dust jacket and the weirdest-coloured food inside. I thought this ingenious idea should resurface. You'll need a good, large crusty loaf, not the pale, soft and weedy type that people give to 1-footed pigeons.

Serves 2

1 crusty white tin or farmhouse loaf,
    a day-old 1 is perfect
4 free-range hard-boiled eggs
assorted vegetables, such as radishes,
    baby carrots, cherry tomatoes, celery
    sticks and cucumber

MAYONNAISE
2 large free-range egg yolks
1 heaped teaspoon Dijon mustard
¼ teaspoon caster sugar
1½ tablespoons white wine vinegar
    or lemon juice
200ml sunflower oil
flaked sea salt and ground black pepper

Place the loaf on its side on a board, then carefully slice off the top and put to one side. Upright the loaf again. Place a knife about 2.5 cm from the outside and cut into the bread down all 4 sides. Pull the bread from inside.

To make the mayonnaise, put the egg yolks, mustard, sugar and vinegar in a high-sided bowl. Whizz with a stick blender while slowly dribbling in the oils together until the mayonnaise thickens and becomes smooth and glossy. Add salt and pepper to taste. Spoon into a small jam jar and fasten the lid. Put the jar inside the loaf of bread and add the hard-boiled eggs. Scrub the vegetables and cut into small batons where necessary. Arrange alongside the mayonnaise and eggs. Wrap some sea salt and ground black pepper individually in small envelopes of foil and add to the parcel.

Pop the bread lid back on and secure with a large elastic band or good string, then disappear on your picnic whence you will return with only the empty jar, elastic band and foil. I guarantee your friends will be amazed.

TOMATO KETCHUP

Life without ketchup would be a sorry thing. It hurts the sensibilities
of certain cooks when you add it to a dish. But if only they realised that
blobbing it about means that you can finish even a bad shepherd's pie as
if in rapturous delight!

Bear in mind when choosing the tomatoes for ketchup that bruised
and battered ones (known as 'seconds'), which should be going for a song in
the market, are a wise buy.

Makes 1 litre

4kg ripe tomatoes
2 medium onions
4 garlic cloves
250ml cider vinegar
150ml malt vinegar
200g light brown muscovado sugar

1 tablespoon flaked sea salt
1 teaspoon English mustard powder
1 heaped teaspoon ground cloves
1 teaspoon ground allspice
½ teaspoon ground ginger
1 cinnamon stick
1 heaped teaspoon celery salt
1 teaspoon ground white pepper

Roughly chop the tomatoes, then peel and roughly chop the onions relatively
finely. Put both in a large, heavy-based saucepan. Peel and slice the garlic
and chuck it in too. Pour over the vinegars, add the sugar, then add all the
rest of the ingredients. Bring slowly to the boil, stirring to dissolve the sugar.
Cover loosely with a lid. Reduce the heat and leave to simmer gently for
3–3½ hours. Watch carefully and stir regularly, particularly towards the end of
the cooking time, as this is the point at which the mixture could begin to stick.

When it is cooked, the liquid should be well reduced and the tomatoes
pulpy. Remove the pan from the heat and discard the cinnamon stick. Blitz
with a hand blender until as smooth as possible. Ladle the mixture in batches
into a large, fine sieve set above a clean saucepan. Use the bowl of the ladle to
force the mixture through the mesh. Really stir, press and mash it. Discard
the seeds and skin once you know you could not extricate one last drop.

Place the pan over a medium heat and add extra salt or pepper if
necessary. Bring to a simmer, stirring constantly. Watch out for splashes, as
the sauce will bubble, burp and scald like hot lava. Cook for 2–3 minutes, then
remove from the heat.

Meanwhile, sterilise 2–3 bottles. Preheat the oven to 180°C/350°F/
Gas 4. Wash the bottles and stoppers really well and put on a baking sheet
in the oven for 10 minutes. Leave to cool slightly.

Pour the hot sauce through a large funnel into the sterilised bottles.
Bump a couple of times on the worksurface to get rid of any air bubbles and
leave open for around 30 minutes before sealing the lids. Store for at least
a month before using, then keep in the fridge once opened.

RATATOUILLE

This is almost a byword for hideous, watery, vegetable slop that tastes predominately of tinned tomato. Why bother? Well, you should. Upturn such muck against the wall, shouting 'NO MORE!'. Made properly with love and served hot or cold under shaded cover from the sun, ratatouille is a most delicious thing. There are many varying recipes, but the simpler the better.

Serves 10

3 medium aubergines
4 medium courgettes
1 tablespoon flaked sea salt
3 red peppers

4 ripe vine tomatoes
2 medium onions
6 small garlic cloves
12 tablespoons olive oil
1 teaspoon coriander seeds
some fresh basil leaves, to finish

Cut the aubergines into 1 cm cubes and the courgettes into 1 cm barrels. Put them in a colander and scatter with the sea salt. Place some stacked plates on top to help press out the water. Leave to drip over the sink for at least 1 hour. Cut the peppers in half lengthways, cut out the seeds and stalk, then cut thinly from end to end.

Criss-cross the bottoms of the tomatoes and cut out the stalk bases. Steep in just-boiled water and leave submerged for 30 seconds. Pour away the water and peel the tomatoes. Finely chop them, retaining the juice and seeds. Peel, halve and thinly slice the onions. Peel and thinly slice the garlic. Everything is now ready for cooking.

Heat a large heavy-based frying pan. Tip the courgettes, aubergines and red peppers into a large bowl and cover with 4 tablespoons of the olive oil. Mix them together until well oiled. The dry pan must be very hot before you add the vegetables, so that they can brown very quickly; avoid the temptation to cram them in, as this will stop the colouring process – do it in batches if needs be.

When browned, put the vegetables back in the bowl and leave to one side. Bring the remaining olive oil to a medium heat in a large, heavy casserole that you plan to cook the ratatouille in. Add the onions and coriander seeds. Cook until the onions are softened, but do not colour. Reintroduce the fried vegetables and add the tomatoes (juice, seeds and all) and garlic.

Cover with a lid and simmer gently for 40–45 minutes. It is imperative the aubergine be completely cooked, as underdone it will cause an unpleasant itch to the roof of the mouth. Cook for a fraction longer, if needs be.

When done, turn the ratatouille out into the large bowl used earlier and gently fold in any extra salt needed, remembering that you salted some of the ingredients earlier and that when cold the seasoning will be more prevalent. When chilled, stir through some torn basil. It is also nice warm.

BEANS & PEAS

When I was small, my mother gave me a large felt pea pod with a zip. When it was undone, 6 tennis-ball sized peas looked out with smiling faces. That's when my healthy appetite for anything with a pod kicked in.

I can't get enough of beans and peas and even when they are out of season I revert to the tinned, dried and frozen ones. Sunday nights are for baked beans on toast and fried salted broad beans are for the riverbank. Fish fingers are as pointless without peas as cod is without mushies.

Boiled, raw, stewed, in salad – I like them anywhere, in fact. When the summer markets are bursting with fresh peas and beans, the brown paper bags get raced home with love and attention in mind. Things get steamy. I frequently get ticked off with an 'Are you going to pay for those?' by my greengrocer, Alan, as I can't help mindlessly podding his peas into my mouth while visiting his stall.

But broad beans, above all, are my favourite vegetable and during their season my flat is littered with empty pods. The sight of the first baby broads is like gazing on a newborn infant.

Peeled baby broads are the ultimate luxury, but peeling can be unnecessary, as the young skin is tasty. Generally, do it only to impress someone you fancy. However, I always peel them when they are old and large, as the skins can be tough and squeaky.

Pea pods make a good addition to soups, especially combined with the tougher part of asparagus stalks, so think twice before ditching them. Cook, purée and push them through a sieve.

Lastly, I find the crunch of French beans annoying. Personally, I think that, on the whole, they are grossly undercooked. Next time try taking them a little further.

BOBBY BEANS À LA GRECQUE

This was cooked for me by a Greek friend, Jessica, and I immediately scribbled the recipe down on the back of a ciggy packet. It's another wonderful dish and highly recommended with cold, crazy-making retsina and dominoes.

Serves 4

2 medium white-skinned onions
8 fat garlic cloves
6 tablespoons good olive oil, plus extra for finishing the dish
4 very large, ripe beef tomatoes

juice of 1 medium lemon
1 teaspoon caster sugar
2 teaspoons flaked sea salt
ground black pepper
450g bobby beans (green beans)
100ml water
a large handful of fresh dill

Peel the onions, cut in half lengthways and very finely slice. Peel and roughly chop the garlic to resemble assorted teeth. Warm the oil in a large, deep saucepan. Add the onion and garlic, cover and cook very gently until the onion is soft but not coloured, stirring occasionally.

Score the bottom of the tomatoes and cut out the stalk bases. Steep them in boiling water. After 30 seconds, remove them and peel off the skins. Slice the tomatoes thickly. Add the tomatoes, lemon juice and sugar to the pan. Season generously with the salt and a good bombing of black pepper. Bring to the boil, then reduce the heat and simmer gently, without covering, for 20–25 minutes or until the tomatoes have turned to pulp and the obvious watery liquid has gone away. Stir often to prevent the tomatoes from burning on the bottom of the pan.

Cut the tails from the beans (but not the nose, as this is pointless). Add the beans to the tomatoes and stir in the water. You might think me idiotic to put water back in the pot when before you were being told to get rid of it, but the method is more reliable this way. Cover and cook gently for 25–30 minutes or until the beans are totally soft. Remove the lid once or twice to stir the mixture as it cooks.

When the beans are very tender, remove from the heat and turn into a suitable salad bowl. Leave to cool to room temperature. Just before serving, chop the dill and stir it through the beans mixture. Splash liberally all over with more olive oil. These are also delicious chilled, especially spooned next to a tender leg of kid goat.

FRENCH BEANS WITH GARLIC AND ROSEMARY

When the weather is hot and sluggish, and you can't be bothered to move, this is a very fine and suitably light lunch as well as a great accompaniment to fat fish and grilled meats such as the veal chops on page 23.

Serves 4

2 large grabbing-handfuls of French beans
5 large garlic cloves

4 tablespoons olive oil
1 good sprig of rosemary
1 teaspoon flaked sea salt
a splash of red wine vinegar

Top but don't tail the beans, as that beautiful long nose is nothing but good bean, so why in heaven's name pinch it off? Drop the beans into a pot of rolling water and boil for 5 minutes. French beans are so often underdone in the name of crunchiness; they need to be bitey but also cooked. Given the right time you should be able to bend them into an S-shape without them snapping, due to being under- or overcooked. We don't want squeaky.

Plunge the cooked beans into a bowl of cold water with a few ice cubes bumping around in it. This will cool them while retaining their bright green colour. Drain them thoroughly and lay them on some kitchen paper to get them dry. Tip them into a serving bowl.

Peel and then patiently slice the garlic as close to paper-thin as you can get. Heat the oil gently in a small saucepan. Meanwhile, strip the rosemary from its stalk and chop it very finely. Drop the garlic and rosemary into the oil, where it should quietly frizzle. Just when the garlic takes on a hint of ivory colour, take the pan off the heat. Pour all the hot oil over the beans and salt well. With a thumb over the top of the vinegar bottle, splash in just enough so that when mixed and tasted only the slightest edge is apparent. Mix all together thoroughly and serve at once.

BROAD BEANS WITH PATA NEGRA HAM

This salad couldn't be simpler and just so happens to contain all of my favourite things. I make it for 1 because it has always been a singular pleasure. *Pata negra* (air-cured ham made from the black-footed pig, stuffed senseless on acorns) can be found in all good Spanish delis. Less expensive *jamon* works well too.

Serves 2

55g finely sliced *pata negra* or other
   Spanish cured ham, torn
120g podded baby broad beans

1 small garlic clove
1 tablespoon extra virgin olive oil
a splash of sherry vinegar
flaked sea salt
ground black pepper

Ideally, you'll use *pata negra* and it will have been cut in the traditional way – almost shavings the length of your thumb; it is rarely sold machine-sliced in packs. If using Serrano ham, cut it down to the same thumb length but a little wider.

Boil the young broad beans in rapidly rolling water for no more than 3 minutes. Drain in a colander, then plunge under cold running water to cool them immediately. Peel them all if they are not young, as the skins of larger broad beans can be a little tough. If young, peel half of them. Although this isn't totally necessary, it provides a therapeutic couple of minutes and makes the dish prettier with its 2 shades of green.

Combine the beans and ham in a small mixing bowl. Peel and chop the garlic clove to teeny-weeny, then add this. Next, splash in the olive oil and a careless teaspoon of the sherry vinegar. Season carefully with salt, as the ham is salty but the beans need a little help, and with a couple of twists of black pepper. Mix gently and thoroughly. A fine dish to eat while reading the papers at the kitchen table.

RUNNER BEAN CHUTNEY

A fridge without chutney is like a car without a spare tyre. When you need it you're screwed without it. This is one of my favourites and good for the late season glut of large runners, kindly given to me by 2 Aussie ladies who run a café in North Cornwall.

Makes 4 x 500ml jars

4 medium onions
250ml malt vinegar
1kg runner beans
1 heaped tablespoon English
    mustard powder

1 heaped tablespoon ground turmeric
25g cornflour
250ml white wine vinegar
250g granulated sugar
2 heaped tablespoons wholegrain
    mustard
2 teaspoons flaked sea salt

Peel and chop the onions into a small dice. Tip into a large, heavy-based saucepan and pour over the malt vinegar. Bring to a gentle simmer, cover loosely and cook for 15 minutes until softened, stirring once or twice.

While the onions are cooking you can prepare the beans. Trim the ends, then cut down each side to remove any strings. Place each bean flat on the board and slice thinly lengthways on a long diagonal into 7 or 8 strips. How many slices you end up with will depend on the size of each bean. Ignore any that have plump little beans hiding within, as they will be the toughest. Plunge the beans into a large pan of boiling water and return to the boil. Cook for 3 minutes, then drain in a colander and refresh under cold water. Drain.

Mix the mustard powder, turmeric, cornflour and 4 tablespoons of the white wine vinegar until smooth.

When the onions are ready, stir in the sugar and remaining white wine vinegar. Bring to the boil and cook for 2 minutes. Add the beans and simmer gently for 10 minutes, stirring occasionally. Stir the cornflour mixture until smooth once more and then pour slowly into the onions and beans, stirring vigorously to dispel any lumps, followed by the wholegrain mustard and salt.

Gently simmer the vegetables, mustard and spices for 20 minutes, stirring regularly so that the chutney does not stick to the bottom of the pan and burn. Pot the chutney into warm, sterilised jars (*see* page 161) and leave to cool. Cover, seal and store in cool dark place for at least a month.

PEA, SALTED YOGHURT AND MINT SALAD

This delightfully easy, quick and fresh lunch can be thrown together with peckish impatience in minutes. Having said that, it does require some strained salted yoghurt to be on standby.

Serves 2–3

200g freshly podded peas
1 long red chile
1 garlic clove
juice of ½ lemon

½ tablespoon extra virgin olive oil
flaked sea salt and ground black pepper
100g firm home-made salted strained
    yoghurt (*see* page 138) or fresh soft
    goat's cheese
a small handful of fresh mint leaves

Bring a small saucepan of water to the boil. Add the peas and return to the boil. Cook for 2 minutes. Drain, then plunge the peas into a large bowl of iced water and leave until cold.

Deseed the chile and chop into tiny pieces. Rubber gloves here would be a wise protection from wandering chile fingers. Peel the garlic and cut into tiny pieces.

Drain the peas and put in a serving bowl. Add the chile, garlic, lemon juice and olive oil. Season with salt and plenty of black pepper and toss together thoroughly.

Break the strained yoghurt (or cheese) into mouthfuls and scatter over the peas. Add the mint leaves, roughly torn. Turn through the peas until lightly mixed and serve.

SUMMER SALAD

This just sings summer, sunshine, gardens, outdoor eating, chirping swallows … it's so fresh, gentle, pleasing and gratifyingly healthy.

Serves 4

300g baby carrots
250g podded baby broad beans
1 bunch of radishes with tops
100g freshly podded peas
a small handful of fresh mint
6 lemon balm leaves (optional)
a small bunch of fresh chives
a large handful of fresh, young curly
    parsley leaves

1 baby gem lettuce or similar amount
    of preferred leaves

VINAIGRETTE
2 tablespoons white wine vinegar
2 good teaspoons Dijon mustard
1 heaped teaspoon caster sugar
a good pinch of flaked sea salt
3½ tablespoons sunflower oil
3½ tablespoons olive oil
ground black pepper

Wash but don't peel the carrots and leave a tiny green tuft at the stalk. Half-fill a small saucepan with water and bring to the boil. Add the beans and cook for 2–3 minutes until tender. Remove with a slotted spoon to a colander, cool under running water and then peel. Cook the carrots in the boiling water for 4 minutes until just tender. Drain and rinse under running water until cold. Peel the beans and carrots in a salad bowl.

Remove the leaves from the radishes, adding the good leaves to the salad bowl and discarding the damaged ones. Cut all but the tiniest radishes in half and chuck them all in. Pod the peas and put them uncooked into the bowl. Strip the mint leaves from their stalks, tear and add them to the bowl, along with the torn lemon balm, if using. Snip the chives in half, chop the picked parsley leaves and scatter both over the salad. Wash and roughly tear the lettuce leaves, then add to the bowl.

To make the vinaigrette, whisk the vinegar, mustard, sugar and salt in a bowl until smooth. Gradually whisk in the oils until the dressing becomes thickened, glossy and emulsified. Season with more salt, if necessary, and a couple of twists of black pepper.

Spoon some dressing over the salad and toss together well. Joy!

ENGLISH GARDEN SOUP WITH PRAWNS

Green is my favourite colour, but that is not why this soup is good. This is certainly a very English-feeling soup and one I can only describe as gentle and calming. The prawns are not a necessity, but are nonetheless happy here, and the pink and green are very pretty together.

This soup should be eaten cold and preferably outside on a hot day. If there is no sorrel available, the soup is still good without it – but add a squeeze of lemon.

Serves 2–3

a couple of handfuls of frozen cooked
   North Atlantic prawns (optional)
1 large banana shallot or 1 small onion
1 fat garlic clove
25g butter
1 medium cucumber

a good grating of nutmeg
flaked sea salt and ground
   white pepper
220g freshly podded peas
200ml good chicken stock, ideally fresh
1 soft, round lettuce
8 large sorrel leaves
2 tablespoons crème fraîche

If you decide to use the prawns, simply shake into a bowl and leave at room temperature to defrost. This should take around an hour. Keep the juice.

Peel and finely chop the shallot and garlic. Melt the butter in a medium saucepan and gently fry the shallot (or onion) and garlic for about 8 minutes or until very soft but not coloured, stirring regularly.

Peel the cucumber and cut in half lengthways. Furrow out the seeds with a teaspoon and discard. Roughly slice each cucumber half and tip into the pan with the shallot and garlic. Add the nutmeg and season well with salt and white pepper. Cook over a medium heat for 3–4 minutes until soft and translucent, stirring occasionally.

Tip the podded peas and stock into the pan and bring to a simmer. If including the prawns later, tip in their juice now. Cover and cook gently for about 7 minutes or until the peas are soft, adding a little more stock if necessary. Don't boil everything to dead khaki.

Separate the lettuce leaves, keeping the stalk, but trimmed of its brown end. Rinse the lettuce and sorrel thoroughly in a colander, drain and roughly chop. Remove the pan from the heat and leave to cool a little before puréeing in a blender until as smooth as possible. Allow to cool in the blender until warm. Blitz again, this time dropping in the lettuce, its stalk and the sorrel leaves. These will add their delicate tastes and fresh colour, but not if the stock is too hot. Pass the green soup through a fine sieve into a serving bowl. Whisk in the crème fraîche. Chill until properly cold.

Adjust the seasoning with more salt and ground white pepper as required and ladle the soup into shallow bowls. Gently lay the prawns on top so that they float. Refreshment is served.

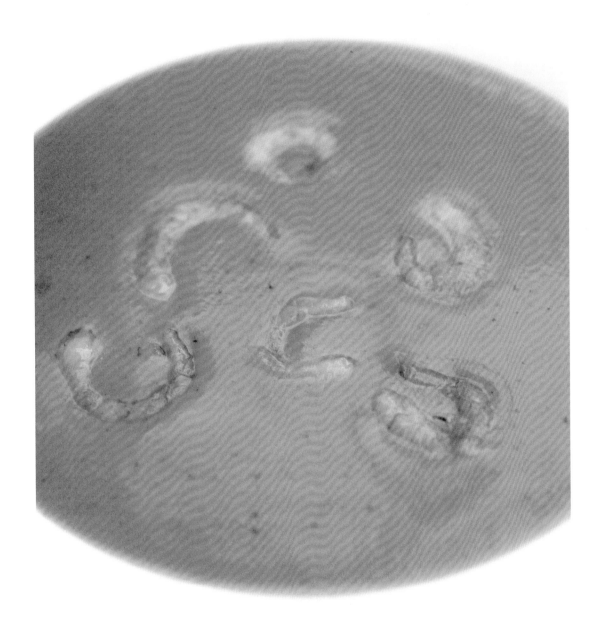

ARTICHOKE ALLA ROMANA

Dipping the fleshy lobes of an adult artichoke into creamy vinaigrette is a simple pleasure, but try them too when young, braised in white wine with good olive oil and eaten cold. This is a most refreshing clean and classy treatment. Steamed fillets of Dover sole could be hard pushed to find a better seat and oversized croûtons scratched all over with garlic are also good for carrying these riders. Try to select young artichokes with a good 5cm of stalk.

Serves 4–5

4 medium carrots
1 medium onion
4 garlic cloves
2 celery sticks
1 teaspoon fennel seeds
1 teaspoon coriander seeds
3 bay leaves

6 black peppercorns
300ml good white wine
1 teaspoon caster sugar
flaked sea salt
8 small globe artichokes
juice of 2 lemons
100ml water
extra virgin olive oil
a handful of chopped flat leaf parsley leaves

Peel the carrots and chop them into the size of small board-game dice. Peel and finely slice the onion and garlic. De-string the celery and chop it into thin slithers. In a heavy-based and lidded flameproof casserole, dry-fry the fennel and coriander seeds until the latter begin to pop, then throw in all the prepared vegetables, the bay leaves, peppercorns, wine, sugar and salt to taste, and leave to one side.

Before dealing with the young artichokes, be sure to don rubber gloves, as preparing this tasty thistle will leave your hands bitter in a way that reminds me of the foul aloes cruel parents painted on my little sucker thumb. Pull off the outer leaves of each artichoke until the greeny-pink ones have gone and only the pale inner ones remain. Cut through the top half of the leaves and discard. Use a teaspoon to scrape out the middle of the petal cup and chuck the velvety fluff. With a potato peeler, skin the stringy stem and nip off the end with a knife. Split the artichokes lengthways in 2, then thoroughly rub them with the lemon juice – this is essential to stop them discolouring. Nestle the pieces in the casserole with the vegetables, add the water and poach on a very gentle simmer, lid on, for 25–30 minutes or so until tender. They should offer no resistance to a probe with a knife.

Remove the lid and allow them to cool before splashing over a good amount of excellent olive oil and a good scattering of chopped parsley. Good with barbecued meats and steamed fish.

LEFTOVERS: Separate the artichokes from the vegetables and liquid, and fry them hard in olive oil with some soaked and drained porcini mushrooms. Dress with a little lemon juice and finely chopped raw garlic. Great eaten with fish or lamb.

POTATOES

FRENCH FRIES

I do not like fat chips and hate them when they are preceded with the words 'hand-cut'. Big deal! I only want to know when they have been cut by the hands of a ring-tailed lemur; that would be interesting.

The ubiquitous chip should be no fatter then those found in vinegar-sodden newspaper, and not stacked and resembling Jenga pieces. French fries are my favourite – slender and crisp. Blobbed in mayonnaise or resting in a salty little pile next to a fat rib-eye, they are the summer chip.

Serves 3

4 large Maris Piper potatoes

sunflower oil, for deep-frying
flaked sea salt
mayonnaise, to serve

Peel the potatoes, then cut the fries the length of the potato and the width of a doll's house kitchen table leg. Wash them under cold water before draining them thoroughly. It is important not to take water into the hot oil.

Heat the oil in your fryer, or alternatively in a saucepan, to 140°C (275°F), and cook the chips for 3 minutes. Move them gently to prevent them from clumping together. Lift them from the oil with a slotted spoon and place them in a colander lined with kitchen paper.

Turn up the heat to 180°C (350°F)and when the oil has reached this temperature, drop in the fries again, cooking them for 5 minutes. They should be straw golden in colour. Turn off the oil and remove the chips to a bowl lined with kitchen paper.

Toss the fries with a good amount of salt before plunging them into mayonnaise and cramming them into your mouth.

POTATO SALAD WITH QUAIL'S EGGS, CAPERS AND ANCHOVIES

I get excited at the mere sight of a glossy handsome potato salad and start fingering the buffet. There is just no excuse for a bad one (cubes of overboiled baking potato in sour mayonnaise) – which is worryingly easy to find next to wrinkly vinegared-beetroot in sandwich shops. Eek! Any small waxy potatoes, my favourite variety being the Pink Fir Apple, are the only entrants for this recipe. The others can go boil their heads.

Serves 6

750g new-season small waxy potatoes,
    such as Charlotte, Jersey or Pink
    Fir Apple, well scrubbed
18 quail's eggs
¼ small red onion
a small handful of fresh chives
3 sprigs of fresh tarragon
a handful of young flat leaf parsley leaves
flaked sea salt and ground black pepper

MAYONNAISE
3 medium free-range egg yolks
1½ heaped teaspoons Dijon mustard
1 teaspoon flaked sea salt
a couple of twists of ground black pepper
juice of 1 small lemon
50ml olive oil
250ml sunflower oil
5 salted anchovy fillets in oil, drained
    (optional)
2 tablespoons baby capers, drained

Put the potatoes in a large pan and cover with cold water. Bring to the boil over a high heat, then reduce the heat and simmer for 15–20 minutes or until tender. Drain in a colander under cold running water. Add the quail's eggs to another small pan of cold water, bring to the boil and cook for 2 minutes. Drain in a sieve under running water until cold.

For the mayonnaise, put the egg yolks, mustard, salt, pepper and lemon juice in a bowl. Whizz with a stick blender until thoroughly blended before slowly, in a thin, thin stream, pouring in the oils. If you find it becomes too thick, and there is still oil to add, just add a tablespoon or 2 of warm water before continuing. If the mayo splits, do not throw it away, but start again with 1 egg yolk, slowly pouring back in the disaster that you created before. Scrape 3–4 large tablespoons of the mayonnaise into a bowl. Roughly chop the anchovy fillets and stir into the mayonnaise with the baby capers.

Slice the potatoes and tip them into a serving bowl. Peel the wee quail's eggs, cut them in half and add to the potatoes. Peel and very finely chop the red onion and scatter over. Strip the whole tarragon leaves from the stems, chop them and the other herbs and add to the salad.

Spoon the mayonnaise on top of the salad and turn with 2 large spoons until all is mixed and evenly coated. Season with a little extra salt and a good grind of black pepper. Plonk on the table.

SPRING ONIONS

CHARGRILLED SPRING ONIONS

In Mexico these are a standard menu item in most *taquerias* (taco houses). As an accompaniment to grilled meats, especially beef, they are outstanding and I now rarely have a barbecue without them. They are also good cooked on a griddle in the kitchen.

Serves 4

12 spring onions

sunflower oil
1 juicy lime
flaked sea salt

Peel away and trim any tatty outer layers or withered tops from the spring onions. Discard. Put the onions in a large bowl. Dribble over a couple of tablespoons of sunflower oil and lovingly grease the onions.

When the hot, grey-orange coals are pulsing out a fierce heat from the barbecue, lay the onions on the grill rack. Watch them, as they will cook quickly. Turn when deeply browned and cook the other side. In all they will need only about 6 minutes. A few blackened tops can always be broken off, but are actually very tasty. Arrange side by side on a plate. Squeeze over the lime juice and sprinkle generously with good sea salt.

LEAVES

Our saviour from overeating, salad is both food and delicious medicine. When I want salad, it is a need like nothing else; I have to have it now.

Whether you like the grown-up bitter tastes of endive, frisée and trevise, or the sweet and joyful nature of butterhead and lamb's lettuce, salad is gently nurturing, like the mother missed and found.

A salad can be straightforwardly simple and cleansing, or a wild forest in a bowl, hiding the unexpected anchovy or sly piece of bacon. And vinaigrette: when was a sauce so suited to its host? There is something about salad and dressing – more than chicken and gravy, or cauliflower and cheese sauce – that goes together.

Whilst enjoying the virtues of raw lettuce, don't overlook the fact that many are excellent when cooked. Blended into chilled summer soups, and wilted and slightly crunchy when hanging out with peas, these leaves are not as faint and fragile as they might at first seem. What a genius is the person who invented caramelised roasted chicory, and the trevise was born to lie on pizza.

ESCAROLE SALAD

My mum makes me this and I love it.

Serves 2

1 escarole lettuce
a good handful of pine nuts

2 garlic cloves, peeled
3 tablespoons olive oil
6 anchovy fillets in olive
   oil, drained
juice of ½ small lemon

Remove the escarole leaves whole from the stalk. Wash them free of grit and disgruntled bugs before drying thoroughly. Roughly tear into a large bowl.

Take a small frying pan and gently colour the pine nuts over a low heat until dark golden. Keep the little fellas on the move so that they do not burn on one side. Tip on to a plate.

Peel and chop the garlic very finely. Heat the olive oil in a frying pan and add the anchovies. The oil should be hot enough to make the anchovies bubble and spit a little, but do not fry hard. Cook until they have collapsed, like the very rotten wood that you might find around the windowsill. Throw in the garlic and very gently fry it until it is the palest golden colour. Turn off the heat and allow to cool for 5 minutes or so.

Tip the pine nuts into the pan and squeeze in the lemon juice before swirling the whole lot around and pouring over the leaves. Mix through the salad leaves and serve immediately.

SNAIL, DANDELION AND BACON SALAD

Delicious snails! It's nice to see them appearing on menus here and there.
However slowly.

Serves 2

a handful of dandelion leaves
a handful of mixed baby salad leaves
50g rustic white bread
2 tablespoons olive oil, plus a splash
    for the bacon
a small handful of flat leaf parsley
75g smoked streaky bacon lardons
100g cooked snails, defrosted if frozen
a good splash of red wine vinegar

GARLIC VINAIGRETTE
1 tablespoon freshly squeezed
    lemon juice
2 teaspoons caster sugar
1 level tablespoon Dijon mustard
1 small garlic clove
flaked sea salt and ground black pepper
4 tablespoons olive oil

Wash the leaves and spin them until very dizzy but dry. Put them in a salad
bowl. Preheat the grill to high.

To make the vinaigrette, beat the lemon juice with the sugar and
Dijon mustard in a bowl. Peel and finely chop the garlic and throw it in with
salt and a twist of black pepper. Beat in the oil with a fork until creamy, then
put the vinaigrette to one side.

Tear the bread into small chunks and toss in the olive oil. Scatter over
a baking tray and put under the preheated grill, turning occasionally, until
crisp and browned but ever so slightly chewy. Pick the parsley of its leaves
and finely chop them.

Heat a frying pan and add the splash of olive oil along with the lardons
to help get them going. Fry for 3–4 minutes until coloured, turning often.
Meanwhile, slice the snails in half through the centre. Deglaze the frying pan
with the vinegar. Make sure all the vinegar has burnt off before adding the
snails. Fry until the snails are good and hot before stirring in the parsley.

Tip the snails, bacon and croûtons on to the leaves. Pour over the
vinaigrette and toss all together lightly. Serve at once while all is warm and
before the leaves have a chance to wilt.

RADISH

RADIS AU BEURRE

A radish with bread and butter is one of those modest pleasures that is as nourishing to the soul as tomatoes and salt or salami with gherkins. It was their destiny to find each other for man's joy.

Serves 1

a bunch of radishes

flaked sea salt
fridge-cold unsalted butter
crusty white sourdough bread

Remove the radish stalks and leaves, and rinse the radishes. Reserve the leaves for salads or eating cooked like spinach.

Put the radishes on a plate with a little pile of salt and some cold, hard unsalted butter. Eat all together with a hunk of torn white sourdough. I think it fitting to do the buttering and any cutting with a penknife.

CUCUMBER

CUCUMBER SALAD

This makes for a most refreshing, cooling lunch and something I love to eat with bread, unaccompanied by fish or meats.

Serves 2

1 cucumber
2 heaped teaspoons flaked sea salt
350ml natural live yoghurt
1 garlic clove

½ small red onion
a handful of fresh dill
a small squeeze of lemon juice
extra virgin olive oil
ground black pepper

Peel the cucumber and cut it into very fine slices, as paper-like as possible. Put it in a colander and sprinkle with the salt. Leave over a bowl to drip for 1 hour.

Squeeze the cucumber over the sink to get rid of the excess water and combine with the yoghurt in a serving dish. Peel and finely chop the garlic and onion and add these. Coarsely chop the dill and sprinkle over. Add a small squeeze of lemon juice, to give everything an edge, and an overflowing tablespoon of extra virgin olive oil.

Stir all the ingredients together until well mixed. Season with black pepper. Chill, covered, for 2–3 hours. Dribble with a good slug of olive oil just before serving.

CUCUMBER SANDWICHES

What a dainty sandwich, definitely a nibbler not a muncher! Anchovy paste such as Gentleman's Relish is a delightful addition and, I never thought I would say it, but so is Marmite, faintly dragged over the butter. Here I shall make this teatime snack in its purest version without either.

Serves a few

a lot of butter
1 cucumber

1 level tablespoon flaked sea salt
1 teaspoon white wine vinegar
ground white pepper
as much sliced white bread as you need

Allow the butter to come to room temperature. Skin the cucumber and then grate it into thin discs on a mandoline or slicer, or cut it very thinly with a knife. Put it in a colander and sprinkle over the salt, turning it with your hands to mix well. Leave the cucumber slices to drip over the sink for at least an hour. Rinse it under cold water briefly and then wring it out like socks in the bath, a handful at a time, squeezing until all have given up as much water as they can. Slide it into a bowl, then splash over the vinegar and dust with a little white pepper to taste.

When choosing the bread, I really don't see a problem with cheap bagged white. In fact, in this case I think I would prefer it over some fancy loaf. Just make sure it is thinly sliced. Cut the crusts from the bread and then butter liberally – but don't rip the bread with chunks of cold butter. Gently lay over a good amount of cucumber, making sure it goes right to the edges so as to ensure no nibble is disappointing. Cover with another slice. Slice across twice from corner to corner. Group the triangles and stand them on a plate. Repeat the process until all the cucumber is used up. Now go and put the kettle on.

GREEK SALAD

This never gets the press it deserves – which is not surprising when it is often found in a sandwich shop, withered, splashed with balsamic vinegar and sitting sadly next to Mexican tuna mix. Any proud Greek would hurl this plate of nonsense to the tiles. Eat the following and think again.

Serves 2 as lunch, or 4 with
    fish or meats

3 tablespoons good black olives
90g feta cheese
2 teaspoons cumin seeds
1 large beef tomato
1 large green pepper

1 medium cucumber
1 smallish red onion
a small bunch of fresh mint
1 teaspoon dried oregano
juice of ½ plump lemon
3 tablespoons good olive oil
1½ level teaspoons flaked sea salt
ground black pepper

When choosing the olives, try to get the loose, wrinkly little ones that resemble shrunken heads instead of the smooth, bland types you tend to get in jars. If you have a cherry stoner, well done – use it on the olives. If not, squeeze each olive between thumb and fingers and fiddle out the stone. Put the fruits in a salad bowl.

Try to find a feta with a faint softness, as they are milder (the harder they are, the saltier). Crumble the cheese so that it resembles the size of firelighters rather than smashed-up polystyrene. Add to the salad bowl.

Toast the cumin seeds in a frying pan until their smell hovers in the kitchen, before tipping them into the bowl. Wash the tomato and pepper. Skin the cucumber, split it from end to end and furrow out the seeds with a teaspoon. Lay the 2 parts side by side and chop into half-moons 1cm wide. Add to the bowl.

Delicately cut out the stalk base of the tomato. Halve the tomato and chop it coarsely. Into the bowl it goes. Peel the onion, halve it from top to bottom and slice each half as thinly as your complete concentration allows. Let the onion join the rest. Halve, deseed and thinly slice the pepper, then add to the salad.

Pull the mint leaves from their stalks and chop them briefly, using 3 or 4 cuts. Scatter over the salad and follow with the dried oregano. Squeeze over the lemon juice and splash in the olive oil.

Add the salt and some pepper and fold all together gently. This is delicious with a barbecued shoulder of goat or lamb and chilled retsina.

Val Warner

GRAINS

FLAT BREAD

This is a very simple dough that is versatile and good for outdoor lunches and barbecues. I love watching the breads puff up like blowfish. But beware – they can cause pain; watch out that they don't breathe hot steam on you and scald your skin.

Makes 6–8

450ml warm water
1 x 7g sachet easy-blend dried yeast
1 teaspoon caster sugar

750g strong plain white flour
2 teaspoons flaked sea salt
1 tablespoon olive oil, plus extra
    for oiling

Pour the water into a measuring jug. It should be warm enough to activate the yeast without killing it; I usually mix 150ml just-boiled water with 300ml cold water. Sprinkle over the yeast and stir in the sugar. Leave for about 10 minutes, or until the yeast has a beige foam floating on the surface. Put the flour in a mixing bowl. Crumble over the salt and stir together.

Pour the olive oil on to the yeast mixture and slowly add to the flour, combining everything into a dough. Turn the dough on to a floured board and knead by hand for 5 minutes until it is well combined and elastic. Be careful not to overknead and make the dough tough.

Put the dough in a large, lightly oiled bowl and cover with a clean, damp tea-towel. Leave to rise in a warm place for about an hour, or until doubled in size.

Transfer the dough to a board and knock back a couple of times with your knuckles. Tear into 6–8 pieces and roll out each one until it forms an oval around 5mm thick. Place on a tray lightly dusted with flour and cover loosely with oiled clingfilm. Leave to rest for 5 minutes or so.

Heat a large, non-stick frying pan or flat griddle over a high heat. Add the flat breads in batches and cook for 2–3 minutes on each side until puffed up and golden brown, flipping over with a spatula. Alternatively, cook over a hot barbecue. Wrap in a dry tea-towel to keep warm while the remainder are prepared. Serve the breads whole, then tear into large pieces and spread with something delicious.

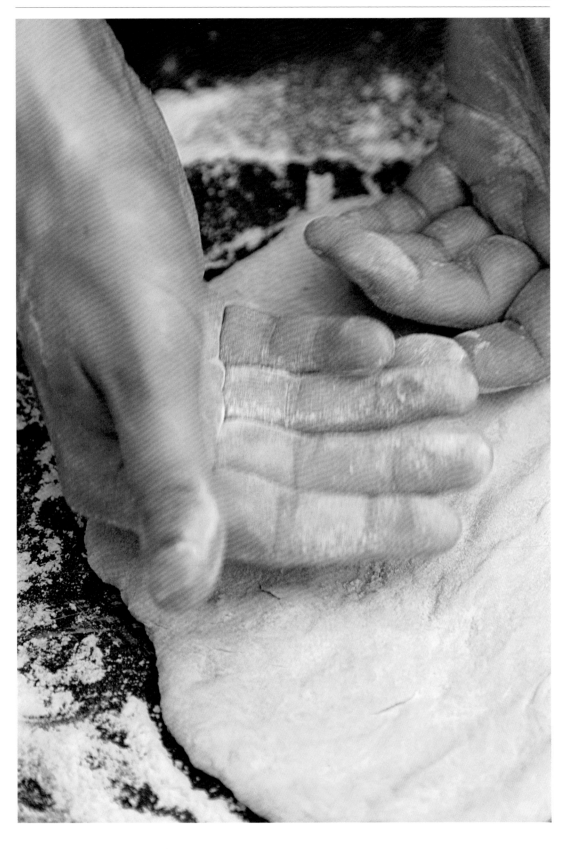

POLENTA AND GIROLLES

Usually I make this with leftover polenta, but it is so delicious that here is a recipe with proportions that are just right to make the dish from scratch.

Serves 2–4

50g Parmesan cheese
250ml water
⅛ teaspoon flaked sea salt
1 bay leaf
50g instant polenta

40g butter, plus 20g for mushrooms
100g girolles
a small handful of young curly parsley
1 fat garlic clove, peeled
2 tablespoons olive oil
a tiny squeeze of lemon juice

Finely grate the Parmesan. Line a 900g loaf tin with clingfilm.

In a medium saucepan, get the water boiling with the salt and bay leaf, then tip in the polenta and stir. Let it cook for 3 minutes, stirring occasionally. When all the water has been absorbed, remove the bay leaf and beat in the 40g butter and Parmesan. Pour the polenta into the lined loaf tin so that it is about 1½cm deep. Leave to cool for at least half an hour.

Meanwhile, remove the dirt, grit or wee beasties from the girolle mushrooms. Wash and dry the parsley, then finely chop it with the garlic and leave to one side.

Turn the cooled polenta out on to a board, trim the edges and cut it in half, then cut each piece into 2 triangles. Get a non-stick frying pan hot before pouring in the olive oil. The pieces of polenta should sizzle immediately on entering the pan. Leave them to fry briskly, regulating the heat so that they colour deeply but do not burn. Cook them for about 5 minutes on each side until they are dark golden and crisp.

Transfer the polenta to warmed plates and immediately throw the mushrooms into the same pan, joined with the extra knob of butter. Fry the mushrooms hard so that any water that seeps out evaporates and they, too, take on a rich nutty colour. All this will take about 5 minutes. Pass over with a tiny squeeze of lemon juice. Scatter over the parsley and garlic, and stir them in, then remove the mushroom mixture from the heat and pile on to the polenta. *Fantastico!*

SHALLOT AND ROSEMARY PIZZA

'What I always tell someone when they want to make bread dough is that, whether they hang on every word of the recipe or not, they'll still end up with bread.' This wise advice, and the dough recipe below, come courtesy of my beautiful friend Martina, a Toronto rock star. When not in a spray-on bodysuit standing behind a synth, she transforms into a homebody pizza queen.

Make 1 small or 2 large pizzas

5 medium banana shallots
3 stalks of rosemary
1 teaspoon flaked sea salt
a tiny pinch of caster sugar
3 tablespoons extra virgin olive oil
ground black pepper

DOUGH
250ml tepid water
1 teaspoon caster sugar
1 x 7g sachet easy blend dried yeast
300g strong white bread flour, plus
   extra for dusting
1 heaped teaspoon flaked sea salt
1 tbsp extra virgin olive oil for greasing

To make the dough, pour the water into a large bowl and gently stir in the sugar and yeast (treat the yeast like a living thing…'cos it is). Put aside for around 10 minutes until the water has a thick beige foam floating on top. Add half the flour and stir gently with a wooden spoon. Don't worry about clumps in the flour, as these will soon disappear.

Gradually add half the remaining flour and continue stirring. Once it is all incorporated, add the remaining flour and the salt, crushing it between your fingers. Mix with clean hands. As soon as the dough forms a soft, spongy ball, turn it out on to a floured surface and knead for 10 minutes. By this time the dough should be smooth, elastic and no longer sticking to your hands.

Put the dough into a lightly oiled bowl, cover loosely with oiled clingfilm and leave to rise in a warm place until doubled in size (45–60 minutes). Turn out the dough on to a lightly floured surface and knock back with mild blows from your fists for a couple of minutes.

Preheat the oven to 240°C/475°F/Gas 9. Tear the dough in half and stretch, or flatten with a rolling pin, until around 25cm in diameter. Place each pizza base on a lightly oiled baking sheet and brush with a little more oil. Cover loosely with oiled clingfilm and leave in a warm place for 20 minutes until puffed up.

Peel the shallots, trim the root end, and halve from tip to toe. Cut each shallot half lengthways into thin slices and transfer to a mixing bowl. Strip the rosemary leaves from the stalks, chop finely and add to the shallots. Sprinkle with the salt and sugar, and pour over 2 tablespoons of the oil. Toss until the shallots glisten with oil. Scatter these and the rosemary over the pizzas. Season with black pepper. Bake for 12–15 minutes (18–20 for 1 large pizza) until risen, golden and crisp. Slide on to a board, dribble with olive oil and either slice elegantly or tear into pieces, making sure that you get more shallot on your bit.

TOMATO AND ANCHOVY PIZZA

This is my favourite pizza and goes something like this. Make the sauce as you would for the arrabiata (*see* page 157), but omitting the lemon juice. When the sauce is ready and cooled, swirl it thinly over the pizza base, then place the anchovies in a circle in a clock formation, with a couple in the middle for good measure. Scatter liberally with dried oregano and streak about with olive oil. Bake for the same time as the shallot and rosemary pizza on page 204, then devour alone in front of the telly.

TABBOULEH

Parsley, for me, is King of Health and constantly I am told that I have something green between my teeth. I eat this all the time in the local Lebanese, with flat bread. It's a modest and boosting lunch.

Serves 4

25g bulgar wheat
2 large, ripe vine tomatoes
a large bunch of fresh flat-leaf parsley

a small bunch of fresh mint
1 small red onion
juice of 1 small lemon
2–3 tablespoons extra virgin olive oil
flaked sea salt

Put the bulgar wheat in a small bowl and cover with 50ml just-boiled water. Stir, then leave to stand for 20 minutes to allow it to absorb the water.

Cut out the green stalk ends of the tomatoes and make a small cross in the bases. Put the tomatoes in a bowl and cover with just-boiled water. Leave for about 30 seconds. Peel – after this time the skins should come away easily. Cut the tomatoes into quarters, discard the seeds and cut the flesh into a small, even dice. Put in a serving bowl.

Rinse the parsley under the tap and, holding it by the stalks, flick out the water (covering the floor and ceiling with a mist of water), then dry thoroughly in a tea-towel or salad spinner. Pick the parsley and mint leaves from their stalks. Chop the leaves finely and add to the tomatoes. Peel the onion and cut it in half, top to bottom, then strip off the skin. Finely chop the onion and add it to the salad. Fluff up the bulgar with a fork to separate the grains and tip into the bowl. The bulgar wheat should be the lesser player in this salad, like 30 sheep in an acre of forest, so to speak.

Squeeze over 2 teaspoons of the lemon juice and add the olive oil. The leaves should look soft and glossy, but not swamped with oil. Season with plenty of salt and toss together well. Add a little more lemon juice or seasoning if needed and serve either with flat bread, for a simple lunch, or grilled meats such as chicken or lamb.

SCONES WITH STRAWBERRY JAM AND CLOTTED CREAM

Ooh! I do love a scone! Accompanied by Darjeeling and the polite tinkling of fine china. Clotted cream or jam first? Well, actually, butter first, then jam – and then cream!

Makes 6 large scones

500g self-raising flour, plus extra
    for dusting
100g butter (at room temperature), plus
    extra for greasing and spreading

a good pinch of flaked sea salt
40g caster sugar
300ml whole milk, plus extra
    for glazing
fresh clotted cream
good-quality strawberry jam

Preheat the oven to 220°C/425°F/Gas 7. Lightly butter a large baking sheet or tray. Sift the flour into a large bowl. Cut the 100g butter into cubes and drop them into the centre of the flour. Rub the flour and butter together until the mixture resembles breadcrumbs. Pinch the salt over, crushing it to tiny flakes. Sprinkle with the sugar and stir in. Slowly add the milk, stirring all the time, until the mixture comes together. Use your hands to lightly knead the dough until smooth. It should be soft and spongy – just verging on sticky. If it feels dry, add a touch more milk.

Turn out the dough on to a floured surface and gently roll it out to around 2.5cm deep. Don't be tempted to roll it any thinner or the scones won't rise as high and look anywhere near as inviting. Use a sharp knife to cut 4 x 7cm squares from the dough. Place on the baking sheet. Lightly knead and re-roll the trimmings, then cut 2 more squares.

Brush the scones with a little milk and bake in the centre of the oven for about 15 minutes until well risen and golden brown. Cool for a short time on the sheet before eating.

Split in half and spread with butter, then thickly with clotted cream. Top with spoonfuls of strawberry jam and eat whilst warm. Life-affirming.

FLOWERS
& A DROP
OF HONEY

ELDERFLOWER

ELDERFLOWER, CUCUMBER AND LIME GRANITA

On a hot day, this rough-and-ready cool green sorbet is even more refreshing than ice-cream.

Serves 6

3 cucumbers
3 very juicy limes
300ml elderflower cordial (*see* page 214)

Peel the cucumbers and cut them into short lengths. Put them in a food processor and blend to a pulp. Pour the pulp into a fine sieve set above a bowl and use a ladle to squeeze the juice from the pulp into the bowl – you should end up with around 450ml. Discard the pulp.

Squeeze the limes. Add the cordial and lime juice to the cucumber liquid and stir well. Try a little on a teaspoon and add a bit more cordial if you can't taste the elderflower. Pour into a freezer-proof container, cover and freeze for 2 hours.

Remove the container from the freezer and scrape the partially frozen mixture with a fork to break up the ice crystals. Return to the freezer. Every 1–2 hours, remove the granita and scrape well with a fork. You'll need to do this about 4 times until the correct texture is reached. By this time the mixture should be pale lime green, with the texture of soft crushed ice-slush.

Once prepared, simply return to the freezer until needed, then either eat or press against your hot brow.

ELDERFLOWER CORDIAL

Elderflowers are magical and I'm sure that the fairies make cordial too. Having my nose stuffed in this heady hedge while collecting the white chandeliers makes me smile as I pick.

Makes roughly 2 x 500ml bottles

25–30 largish unsprayed elderflower heads
1kg granulated sugar

25g tartaric acid
1 large unwaxed or well-scrubbed lemon
750ml just-boiled water

Rinse the flower heads gently and shake over the sink to help get rid of any insects. Snap off any particularly thick stalks connected to the flower heads, leaving just the slim stems holding each blossom. Put the flower heads in a large preserving pan or bowl. Sprinkle with the sugar and tartaric acid.

Peel the lemon rind in wide strips and add to the pan, along with all the lemon juice. Add the just-boiled water and stir well. Cover loosely with a tea-towel and leave to stand in a cool place for 24 hours, stirring every now and then.

The sugar should completely dissolve and the syrupy cordial will become infused with the flavour of elderflowers. Strain the contents of the pan through a muslin-lined colander into a clean bowl. Decant into sterilised bottles (*see* page 161). Seal and store in the fridge for up to 3 months.

LAVENDER

LAVENDER CREAM MERINGUES

These are proper little feather-light confections that I think should be called 'fairy tits'.

Makes 16

3–4 fresh unsprayed lavender stems
2 large free-range egg whites
100g caster sugar

a little purple food colouring (red and
blue colouring pastes mixed), optional
½ tablespoon icing sugar
150ml double cream

Preheat the oven to 130°C/250°F/Gas ½. Line a large baking sheet with baking paper. Strip the lavender from its stems straight into a mortar. Bash determinedly with the pestle for a minute or 2 to break the flowers and release their fragrance.

Put the egg whites in a large, clean bowl. Whisk with electric beaters until stiff but not dry. You should be able to turn the bowl upside down without the egg whites sliding out. Gradually whisk in the caster sugar, just a tablespoonful at a time, until all is incorporated. The meringue should look thick and glossy. Sprinkle over 1 tablespoon of the lavender flowers and whisk them in.

If you'd like your meringues to be an interesting shade of purple to complement the lavender, add a few drops of food colouring (you'll need to mix red and blue). Use a colouring paste designed for icing, as it gives the best result. Dab a little on to the end of a cocktail stick so that you have control over the amount that you are adding. Whisk well and assess the colour. If it is still too pale, add a little more and whisk again. It is better to err on the side of less to begin with, as the colouring is intense.

Spoon the meringue mixture inside a roomy piping bag fitted with a large plain nozzle. Squeezing gently, pipe 32 small meringues on to the lined sheet. Put in the centre of the oven and immediately reduce the temperature to 100°C/225°F/Gas ¼. Bake the meringues for 2 hours until crisp but not coloured. Turn off the oven and leave to cool. Lift the meringues gently from the sheet and store in an airtight tin.

No more than 30 minutes before serving, sift the icing sugar over the cream and whip until fairly stiff peaks form. Spoon a teaspoon of cream on to the underside of one of the meringues and sandwich with a second meringue. Do exactly the same with the remaining meringues. Serve before they have a chance to float off the plate.

ROSE

ROSE PETAL SPONGE

This cake is heaven-sent from the angels' tea trolley. It may be a bit girlie, but, hey, I can live with that. As sponges are not my forte, the following cakey directions are from the excellent Justine Pattison, my tireless kitchen aid. Her sponges float from the plate, whereas mine have been known to dent car doors.

Serves 8

60g butter, plus extra for greasing
4 large free-range eggs, (at room
    temperature)
150g caster sugar
½ teaspoon vanilla extract
115g plain flour
1½ level tablespoons cornflour

FILLING
1 x 284ml carton double cream
roughly 150g rose petal jelly

TOPPING
1–2 teaspoons icing sugar, sifted
frosted rose petals (*see* page 220)

Unless you are lucky enough to own 3 x 18cm loose-based sandwich tins, you'll need to cook the sponges in 2 batches. Preheat the oven to 180°C/350°F/Gas 4. Line the bottom of 2 x 18cm loose-based sandwich tins with baking paper. Butter the tins generously on the bottoms and sides to prevent the cakes from sticking.

Slowly melt the 60g butter in a small saucepan. Put to one side and leave to cool for a few minutes. Break the eggs into a large mixing bowl and add the sugar and vanilla extract. Place the bowl over a saucepan of gently simmering water. Whisk with electric beaters for at least 5 minutes, or until thickened and creamy. The whisk should leave an obvious trail on the surface when lifted from the mixture. Remove from the heat and whisk for a further 5 minutes.

Mix the flour and cornflour in a bowl. Sift roughly half of the mixture over the egg and sugar. Fold it in using a large metal spoon. Pour the cooled butter around the edge of the bowl – it should begin to sink. Sift the remaining flour on to the batter. Fold in both butter and flour together very gently until combined. But don't get carried away. Over-handling at this point will result in a heavy cake.

Divide two-thirds of the mixture between the 2 tins and coax gently to the sides with a rubber spatula, smoothing out the surface. Put the rest of the mixture to one side while the cakes are baked. Place in the centre of the oven and bake for 15–16 minutes, or until well risen and the palest golden brown. After the recommended time, the cakes should be just starting to shrink away

from the sides of the tins, and if you press your finger lightly on the surface of each one, the sponge should spring back without leaving an indentation.

Take the cakes out of the oven and run a knife around each one to loosen. Stand them for a couple of minutes in the tins. Turn them out on to a wire rack, remove the baking paper and leave to cool. Wash and dry the tins. Line the base of one of them with more baking paper and grease the base and sides of the tin with butter. Add the reserved sponge batter and bake in exactly the same way as the first batch.

Once all 3 sponges are cooled, you are ready to assemble the cake. First, whip the cream for the filling until it forms soft peaks. Put the rose-petal jelly in a bowl and stir vigorously with a spoon until it has a soft, spreading consistency. Place 1 of the sponges on a serving plate and spread with half the jelly, taking it right out to the edge. Drop dessertspoonfuls of the cream on top and spread very gently, being careful not to disturb the jelly, again making sure that it goes right out to the edge. Spread a second cake with the remaining jelly and cream. Sandwich with the first, topping uppermost. Finish with the final sponge and dust generously with sifted icing sugar. Decorate with frosted rose petals (*see* below).

Leave the cake in a cool place until ready to serve, then cut into generous wedges – or push whole into the face of your arch enemy.

NOTE: If you can't get hold of rose-petal jelly, good strawberry or raspberry jam will do. Stir 2–3 teaspoons rosewater into the jelly to give it an extra boost.

FROSTED ROSE PETALS

2 undamaged and unsprayed fragrant
   edible roses

1 free-range egg white, very
   lightly whisked
caster sugar

Pick the most fragrant edible roses in your garden and separate the petals. Select the largest well-shaped petals. Snip out the yellow, triangular part of each petal, as this can taste bitter. Put the petals on a small tray lined with baking paper.

Use a paintbrush to brush one side of each petal with the egg white and sprinkle with caster sugar. Leave to harden for a few hours, then turn over and repeat the process on the other side. When all the petals are crisp, put them in an airtight container and seal firmly. They are best used within a couple of weeks.

HONEY

ORANGEY HONEY BUNS

These are very good taken at any time of day with tea. Also excellent for a pudding at 3 o'clock in the morning.

Makes 12

150g plain flour
½ teaspoon flaked sea salt
20g caster sugar
1 x 7g sachet easy-blend dried yeast
3 large free-range eggs, lightly whisked
75g diced butter, softened, plus extra
    for greasing

SYRUP
500g caster sugar
4 long strips of orange rind
500ml cold water
100g good runny honey
4 tablespoons orange liqueur
½ teaspoon orange-flower water
    (optional)

Mix the flour, salt, sugar and yeast in a large bowl. Add half the eggs and whizz with an electric whisk until well mixed and extremely sticky. Gradually add the remaining eggs, alternating them with the butter, and mix to soft dough. Beat with a wooden spoon until smooth.

Spoon the mixture into a well-greased 12-hole muffin tray (I've used one with heart-shaped holes) and leave to rise in a warm place for about an hour or until the mixture doubles in size and reaches to the top of the tin. Preheat the oven to 220°C/425°F/Gas 7.

Bake the buns for 12–14 minutes until well risen and pale golden brown. When they are ready, remove them from the oven and leave them to cool on a wire rack.

While the buns are cooling, make the syrup. Put the sugar in a saucepan with the orange rind and stir in the cold water. Stir over a low heat until the sugar dissolves, then bring to the boil. Boil for 3 minutes. Remove from the heat and stir in the honey, liqueur and orange-flower water, if using. Set aside to cool.

Dip 6 buns in the syrup and serve straight away. Pack the remaining buns into a 1-litre sterilised jar (*see* page 161). Gently pour the just-warm syrup over the buns and leave to stand for 20 minutes. Top up with any remaining syrup as they are thirsty little things. Cover and seal the jar tightly. Keep in the fridge until you want to serve them. The buns should last at least a month in their syrupy bath.

Serve the honey buns with a little of the syrup spooned over and lots of whipped cream.

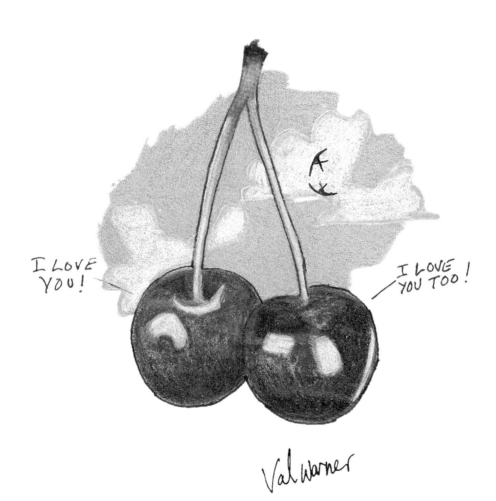

FRUIT

BERRIES & CURRANTS

The whole point of berries, for me, is in them not making it back to the kitchen. It's a schizophrenic tussle between knowing what you need for pud and giving in to the greater urge.

When young and like the cunning blackbird, I would quietly sneak under the fruit nets and into paradise, only to find my brother already there, infuriatingly red-chinned and gorged. Competitive feasting ensued. Then suddenly the wall's door latch would click and we would drop to the ground, holding our breath, with hearts beating like the now-frantic blackbirds trying to flap their way out of prison.

Although the gardener was a terrifying man, no thrashing could ever tarnish the delight of targeting particularly fat raspberries and loganberries, or the special way strawberries, tamed or wild, revealed themselves to searching fingers. Strawberries required skilful hunting, whereas raspberry picking was a blood bath. The taste of those fruits under the summer sky could never be matched by even the finest ones my local market has to offer now.

I loved the cascades of blackcurrants just as much, being possessed with a sour as well as sweet tooth. They have a vitamin tang and punch like nothing else. Once the skin has burst, I physically feel my body grabbing at the tartness, sugar and zing, as if in order to quench its needs. When turned into flavourings – sweets, drinks, jams and other tooth-dissolvers – the blackcurrant holds its identity like no other fruit. They are also excellent with dark-meated game such as pigeon, grouse and venison.

Redcurrants lend their even sharper and most refreshing attitude to puddings and jelly. The white ones, however, simply remind me of foppish Elizabethan earrings.

Imagine an English summer without berries: impossible. Of course, few additions are better than a tip of cream and a dusting of sugar on the chosen fruit, but fresh berry milkshakes make good moustaches and the possibilities for fancy sponges and heavenly ice-creams – my favourite being raspberry ripple – are endless. Remember to replace the obvious strawberry or raspberry every now and then with the blackcurrant. And of course you must go and make yourself a raspberry daiquiri, an excellent evening sharpener with which to stroll round the garden.

SUMMER PUDDING

This is one of the greatest bread puddings ever invented. Summer without this sweet-bleeding delight is no summer at all. To get a well-coloured pudding it should really be made the day before it is to be eaten.

Serves 6

400g raspberries
800g strawberries, hulled and halved
    if large
600g blackcurrants or redcurrants,
    stringed

300g caster sugar
juice of ½ lemon
150ml white wine
300ml water
12 slices of thick-cut white bread
fresh Jersey double cream, to serve

Put half the fruits in a large saucepan with the sugar, lemon juice, wine and water. Bring to a gentle simmer and cook for about 5 minutes until softened, stirring occasionally. Lift out the fruit into a sieve using a slotted spoon, strain any liquid back into the saucepan, then put any fruit in a bowl on one side. Return the pan to the heat and boil the liquid for 20–25 minutes until syrupy.

Strain and reserve 200ml of the fruit syrup. Tip the cooked fruit back into the saucepan. Allow it to cool (this is so you don't cook the raw fruits in the hot ones). Stir in the remaining raw fruit (I like a mixture of cooked and not-cooked for better flavour and texture).

Line a 1.8-litre pudding basin with 2 large sheets of overlapping clingfilm (the edges of the clingfilm should hang over the top of the basin so that they can enclose the pudding). Cut the crusts off the bread and cut each slice into 2 large rectangles. Thoroughly paint 1 side of each rectangle with the reserved syrup. Cut and paint a circle that fits the bottom of the basin. Put this in the basin with the red side facing the clingfilm. Arrange the bread all the way around the inside of the basin, overlapping slightly where the joins meet, with the painted side always facing the clingfilm.

Spoon the fruit into the basin and top neatly with the remaining painted slices of bread, cutting to fit as necessary. Cover with the overhanging pieces of clingfilm and place a side plate holding a heavy weight on top to press it down. Put in the fridge and leave overnight.

When ready to serve, remove the weight, open the clingfilm and invert the pudding on to a serving plate. Remove the clingfilm. Should there be any syrup left, using a pastry brush, daub any pale patches with it. Serve the pudding with cream.

RASPBERRY RIPPLE ICE-CREAM

I love all ice-cream (except 'mackerel dog-biscuit crunch'). Ripples give that added pleasure every time you hit a rich seam. Then the ripple runs out and you have to mine deeper, and then it's just…finished.

Serves 6

600ml double cream
600ml whole milk
1 vanilla pod
10 large free-range egg yolks
225g caster sugar

THE RIPPLE
500g fresh raspberries or blackcurrants
50g caster sugar
3 tablespoons water

To make the ice-cream, pour the cream and milk into a large saucepan. Cut the vanilla pod in half lengthways and scrape out the seeds with the point of a knife. Whisk the seeds into the pan and add the pod. Bring to the boil, then immediately turn off the heat. Remove the vanilla pod and wash well. Allow it to dry and keep it, as it can be used to flavour sugar and subsequently future ice-creams and puddings.

Whisk together the egg yolks and caster sugar until pale. Pour in the milk and cream mixture, whisking immediately. When thoroughly combined, return the liquid to the saucepan and set over a low heat.

Cook for 15–20 minutes, stirring constantly, until the custard is thick enough to coat the back of the spoon. This custard stage needs your total commitment; you must robotically stir at all times. Do not allow it to overheat or the egg yolks will begin to scramble. (This can possibly be salvaged by pouring the mix through a fine sieve; if after sieving it is still grainy, you will have to start again.) Remove the pan from the heat and pour the custard into a clean bowl. Cover the surface with clingfilm to stop a skin from forming. Leave to cool for 30 minutes.

While the custard is cooling, make the raspberry ripple sauce. Rinse the fruit and put it into a large saucepan with the sugar and water. Bring to the boil, then simmer rapidly for about 10 minutes until the fruit has totally collapsed. Put a sieve over another small saucepan and tip in the contents, gently pressing while stirring. Return to the heat and simmer gently until reduced. It wants to be the consistency of cough mixture. Do not allow it to overcook or it will become too jammy, or undercook, as when frozen it will add a water-crystal element to an otherwise creamy luxury. Leave to cool.

Pour the cooled custard into an ice-cream machine and churn for about 40 minutes until it is very thick and smooth. Spoon roughly a third of the ice-cream into a lidded freezer-proof container.

Top with generous spoonfuls of the raspberry sauce, then add more ice-cream. Continue in loose layers until all the ice-cream and sauce are used up. Take a table knife and swirl it very lightly through the ice-cream to roughly marble the sauce through the mixture. Cover with the lid and freeze until solid.

Remove from the freezer and leave to stand at room temperature 10 minutes before serving. Eat in the sun in joyful ignorance that you are dripping it all over your T-shirt.

RASPBERRY, PEACH AND ALMOND TART

Kind of a peach melba affair, with frangipane that is a wonderful vehicle for these harmonious fruits.

Serves 8–10

PASTRY
250g plain flour, plus extra for dusting
150g fridge-cold unsalted butter,
    cut into small pieces
1 tablespoon caster sugar
1 medium free-range egg
1 tablespoon cold water

FILLING
4 firm, ripe peaches

5 tablespoons good-quality raspberry jam
175g unsalted butter, softened
175g golden caster sugar
125g ground almonds
65g plain flour
½ teaspoon flaked sea salt
½ teaspoon baking powder
2 medium free-range eggs, beaten
¼ teaspoon vanilla extract
a large handful of raspberries
a large handful of flaked almonds

To make the pastry, put the flour, butter and sugar in a food processor and blend until the mixture resembles fine breadcrumbs. Beat the egg with the water and add to the mixture while the motor is running. Stop blending as soon as it forms a ball. Roll out the pastry on a lightly floured worksurface and use to line a deep, non-stick fluted flan tin that is 25cm wide. Lightly prick the base with a fork. Put on a sturdy baking tray and chill for 30 minutes. Preheat the oven to 200°C/400°F/Gas 6.

Line the pastry case with baking paper and fill with baking beans. Bake blind for 20 minutes, then remove the paper and beans. Return to the oven for a further 4 minutes until the base is dry. Remove from the oven and put to one side while the filling is prepared. Reduce the oven temperature to 170°C/325°F/Gas 3.

Rinse the peaches, cut them in half and remove the stones. Don't bother to peel off the skin. Set the fruit aside. Spread the jam gently and evenly over the pastry case, right up to the corner.

In a food processor, blend together the butter and sugar until they are creamed. Next, add the ground almonds, flour, salt, baking powder, eggs and vanilla extract. Blend well. Spoon the almond mixture on top of the jam, working it around the outside before heading towards the middle of the pastry case. Smooth the surface with a spatula.

Place 7 peach halves, cut-side down, around the tart and 1 half in the middle, pressing gently into the almond batter. Dot the tart with raspberries, pushing them into the frangipane around the peaches. Don't worry about the fruit sitting on top, as the almond filling will rise snugly around it.

Bake for 30 minutes. Sprinkle all over with the flaked almonds and return to the oven for a further 20–25 minutes until the peaches are tender and the topping well risen and golden brown. Leave to stand for 15 minutes before lifting from the tin. If you wish, carefully pinch off the wrinkled peach skins and discard. Serve warm or cold in generous wedges with cream.

STRAWBERRY CREAM FANCIES

Every now and then I do like a sweet fancy, so here is one. Please excuse the cat on the table (it was hard to resist framing this cute scene with a misty border).

Makes 8

600g small fresh strawberries

BISCUITS (makes 16)
225g strong plain flour, plus extra
    for rolling
1 tablespoon icing sugar, plus
    about 4 teaspoons for baking
    and extra for dusting
a good pinch of fine sea salt
185g butter

125ml cold water
2 teaspoons lemon juice

CRÈME PÂTISSIÈRE
4 large free-range egg yolks
75g caster sugar
10g plain flour
10g cornflour
250ml whole milk
½ vanilla pod, cut in half lengthways
150ml double cream

To make the biscuits, sift the flour, icing sugar and salt into a large bowl. Cut the butter into roughly 2cm pieces and drop into the flour. Toss around with a large metal spoon until the butter is lightly coated in the flour. Mix the water and lemon juice and pour into the flour and butter. Use a table knife to cut across the bowl several times, chopping the butter into the flour until the dough comes together. When it forms a loose lump, tip it on to a board and quickly shape it into a fat slab.

    Flour the worksurface well and roll out the dough to a rectangle around 38 x 20cm using a well-floured rolling pin. Fold the bottom one-third of the dough two-thirds of the way up the pastry rectangle, then fold the other third over that. Press the edges firmly with the pin, then rotate the pastry a quarter turn. Use the rolling pin to make 3 shallow depressions horizontally across the pastry – this will help to keep the edges straight. Roll into the same size rectangle and start the process again. Continue 5 more times: rolling to the same size rectangle, folding, pressing, turning a quarter-turn and making the depressions. Don't worry too much if the butter makes its way through occasionally in the early stages; just keep the board and pin very well floured to prevent the pastry from sticking.

    After the last folding stage, wrap the slab in clingfilm and chill for 1 hour. If it is very firm when you come to use it, allow the pastry to warm through for a few minutes before rolling. Cut the pastry in half and roll out 1 section to a 20 x 30cm rectangle. Roll tightly from 1 long side into a long, fat sausage shape. Cover with clingfilm and chill for several hours or overnight. Do exactly the same with the other piece, but wrap this one well in foil and freeze it for using another time. It will freeze well for up to 3 months.

To bake the biscuits, preheat the oven to 190°C/375°F/Gas 5. Trim the chilled pastry roll and cut it into 16 slices, each 1cm thick. Roll each of these out on a lightly floured surface until 3mm thick. Place 8 biscuits on a sturdy baking tray lined with baking paper, evenly spaced apart (a solid, well-made tray will help them to cook more evenly). Sprinkle with 2 teaspoons sifted icing sugar. Cover with a second sheet of baking parchment and place a second tray, base-side down, on top of the biscuits to stop them from rising. Bake in the centre of the oven for 10 minutes or until rich golden brown. Leave to cool on a wire rack. Repeat with the remaining 8 biscuits.

To make the crème pâtissière, put the egg yolks and caster sugar in a bowl and whisk with electric beaters until pale and creamy, then whisk in the flour and cornflour until smooth. Put the milk in a medium saucepan. Scrape the vanilla seeds out of the pod into the milk and bring to a simmer.

Remove from the heat and gradually add to the egg mixture, whisking constantly with a large metal whisk. Tip into the saucepan and cook for 8–10 minutes, stirring constantly, until thickened and creamy. There shouldn't be any floury taste remaining. Pour into a large bowl and cover the surface with clingfilm to prevent a skin forming and leave to cool.

Now the dessert is ready to be assembled. Whip the double cream into peaks and gently fold it into the cooled custard. Hull the strawberries and turn on to the stalk ends. Cut each one into 5–6 vertical slices, keeping the original shape. Place a biscuit on a serving plate or cake stand and top with a tablespoon of the custard. Arrange the cut strawberries on top. Add another generous spoonful of the custard and sit a second biscuit jauntily on top. Follow the same method until you have made 8. Dust with more icing sugar and serve at once.

These cannot be prepared too far ahead as they will eventually become soggy, but they take only a few minutes to assemble once you have the essentials to hand.

BLACKCURRANT CREAM

What on earth possessed me to include this, I don't know. I cannot take this pudding seriously – it just gives me the giggles. Nonetheless, this mad, wobbling breast of a thing is delicious.

500g fresh blackcurrants, plus a handful
  to decorate
100g caster sugar, plus extra if needed
3 tablespoons water

3 tablespoons crème de cassis
6 sheets of gelatine (12g)
350ml double cream, plus extra to serve
350ml whole milk

Strip the blackcurrants from their stalks with a fork and put in a saucepan with the sugar and water. Cook gently for 10 minutes or until well softened, stirring often. Remove from the heat and press the berries through a fine sieve to make a smooth purée. You should end up with about 300ml. Stir in the cassis and set aside.

Put the gelatine sheets in a bowl and cover with cold water. Set aside for 5 minutes to soften. Heat the cream and milk in a saucepan until it almost comes to a simmer and immediately remove from the heat. Lift the gelatine sheets from their bath and squeeze out the excess water. Plop the gelatine into the cream, stirring until it dissolves into the warm liquid.

Rinse a 1-litre jelly mould or basin with cold water. Stir the cream into the puréed blackcurrants until smooth and sweeten with a little extra sugar if you feel it needs it. Pour carefully into the mould. Cover with clingfilm and chill for 7–8 hours until set.

To serve, remove the clingfilm and dip the mould into a large bowl of just-boiled water until it reaches nearly all the way up the side. Count slowly to 5, then lift out and press your fingertips around the edge of the cream to break the seal. Invert directly on to a serving plate. Give the mould a hard downwards jerk and the pudding should release itself with a satisfying slurp. If not, repeat the process. Take care not to leave the mould in hot water for too long or you'll end up with a melted blob.

Serve decorated with fresh blackcurrants – and some leaves too, should you have them. Add a dribble of cream.

RHUBARB

BREAKFAST RHUBARB WITH GINGER

My fried breakfast programming is broken with a flash of electric pink when the spring rhubarb session starts. Ginger and rhubarb were born to be lovers. I like this with goat's yoghurt.

Serves 4

7 medium stems of fresh pink rhubarb
a thumb-sized piece of fresh root ginger

4 tablespoons runny honey
freshly squeezed juice of ½ orange
yoghurt, to serve

Trim the rhubarb and rinse it in cold water – the little beads of water that cling on and the orange juice are all you need to poach the stems perfectly. Cut each rhubarb stem into 6 lengths and put in a saucepan. Peel and finely slice the ginger (if cut too large it is not pleasant to eat and will end up in the bin). Add the ginger to the rhubarb. Drizzle with the honey and pour over the orange juice.

Cover the pan and cook over a low heat for about 10 minutes until the rhubarb is tender but not breaking apart; a sharp knife inserted into one of the pieces should slide in with no resistance. Don't be tempted to stir or prod the rhubarb as it cooks or it will quickly turn to mush – just give the pan a shake now and then.

Remove the pan from the heat and, using a slotted spoon, carefully transfer the rhubarb to a small serving dish. Return the pan to the heat, bring to the boil, and cook for 3–4 minutes until syrupy. Allow to cool. Pour the sauce over the rhubarb and serve with lots of yoghurt.

CHERRIES

CHERRY PIE

On the whole I think cherries should not be cooked, but rather eaten in a hammock and from a bowl, the fruit covered in clinging droplets of the water they were rinsed under. Having said that, there are exceptions. Cherry drops, cherry jam but, best of all, cherry pie. Remember to load the shotgun in case some thieving hands appear from below the window lintel.

Serves 6

FILLING
750g fresh cherries (ideally the red ones)
150g good-quality black cherry jam
100ml water, plus 2 tablespoons for
   the arrowroot
1 tablespoon ground arrowroot

PASTRY
250g plain flour, plus extra for dusting
175g fridge-cold unsalted butter,
   cut into cubes
1 tablespoon caster sugar, plus
   2 teaspoons for dredging
1 large free-range egg
1 tablespoon cold water

To make the filling, remove the cherry stalks and flick out the stones (use a cherry stoner if you have one, but if not cut the cherries almost in half to ease out the stones). Put the fruit to one side.

Spoon the cherry jam into a small saucepan and add the 100ml water. Heat gently, stirring constantly, until the jam melts and begins to bubble. Mix the arrowroot with 2 tablespoons cold water to form a smooth paste and stir into the pan. Return to the heat and simmer gently, stirring constantly, until the sauce is very thick and smooth. Tip all the cherries into the pan and turn them to coat in the sauce. It will look very sticky, but this is correct; as the cherries cook, they will release more of their juice into the sauce. Transfer to a roughly 1-litre pie dish, piling up well above the rim. Leave to cool.

To make the pastry, put the flour, butter and sugar in a food processor and blend until the mixture resembles fine breadcrumbs. In a bowl, lightly whisk the egg with the 1 tablespoon cold water. Put 1 tablespoon of the egg mixture (to glaze the pie) in a separate small dish. Add the rest slowly to the flour mixture while the motor is running. Stop blending as soon as it begins to form a ball.

Squidge the pastry into a lump and place it on a lightly floured surface. Roll out with a floured rolling pin to around 7cm larger than the rim of the pie dish. Cut 2 or 3 long, 2.5cm-wide strips from the edges. Brush the rim of the pie dish with a little of the reserved beaten egg and place the strips around the circumference, overlapping slightly at the joins. This will help to make a thicker edge for crimping. Brush the pastry rim with more egg and gently lift the remaining rolled pastry over to cover the filling and rim. Press firmly to seal the 2 layers of pastry together, then neatly trim off the excess and crimp the edges with your fingertips. (You can use any pastry trimmings to make decorations for the pie or use for jam tarts.) Place the pie on a sturdy baking tray and chill for 30 minutes. Preheat the oven to 200°C/400°F/Gas 6.

Brush the pastry with the remaining egg glaze and sprinkle with the 2 teaspoons sugar. Make a small hole in the centre of the pie with the point of a knife and bake for 25–30 minutes. Reduce the heat to 180°C/350°F/Gas 4 and continue cooking for a further 15–20 minutes until the pastry is golden brown and glistening. Serve hot with proper custard or cream.

APRICOTS

APRICOT UPSIDE-DOWN TART

This tart was so delicious that, when tried for the first time, two of us ate the whole thing in 20 minutes flat. It should be called 'apricot face-down tart' for the memory of lying on the grass groaning in post-piggish discomfort.

This tart has a rich, sweet pastry that can prove problematic when handling, so you'll need to have a couple of sheets of baking paper to help you to roll it out without breaking the dough.

Serves 6

7–9 fresh apricots, depending on size
15g unsalted butter
1 teaspoon caster sugar

PASTRY
235g plain flour
a small pinch of flaked sea salt

170g fridge-cold unsalted butter
50g caster sugar
1 large free-range egg
1 tablespoon water

BUTTERSCOTCH
100g caster sugar
50ml water
40g butter

Preheat the oven to 200°C/400°F/Gas 6. To make the pastry, put the flour and salt in a food processor and add the chilled butter, cut into rough chunks. Sprinkle over the sugar and blend on the pulse setting until the mixture resembles fine breadcrumbs. Beat the egg and water together and, with the motor running, pour just enough on to the flour mixture to form a pastry ball. Blend until the pastry forms a ball. (If you don't have a food processor, simply rub the butter into the flour by hand, stir in the sugar and then stir in the liquid, first with a table knife, then by hand.) Turn out the pastry on to a large sheet of baking paper. Cover with a second sheet and roll out to a circle about 25cm wide, using a dinner plate or round cake tin to help you to trim it into a neat shape. Put to one side while the butterscotch is prepared.

For the butterscotch, put the sugar and water in a small, ovenproof frying pan and cook over a low heat until the sugar dissolves. Increase the heat to fairly high and simmer, without stirring, for about 5 minutes. At this point the sugar syrup should have begun to change colour. Swish the liquid around the pan a couple of times and continue simmering until the caramel turns a golden-brown. While the caramel is cooking, cut the apricots in half and take out the stones. Remove the pan from the heat and add the butter. Take care as the caramel will foam and bubble with larval ferocity at this stage. Stir well until the butter melts and forms a soft, smooth fudge-coloured butterscotch. Leave to stand for 5 minutes.

Place the apricots, cut-side down, in the warm butterscotch.
Gently lift the pastry on top and loosely tuck down the sides, into the pan
with a round-bladed knife. Prick the surface all over with a fork and dot
with the last 15g butter. Sprinkle evenly with the caster sugar and place the
pan in the centre of the oven. Bake for 25–30 minutes until the pastry is
golden and cooked.

Remove the pan from the oven. Leave to cool for 5 minutes. Loosen
the edge with a knife, then invert on to a serving plate. Be careful, as the pan
handle will be very hot. Serve warm or cold in generous wedges and with
plenty of cream or the raspberry ripple ice-cream on pages 232–3. Yippee!

PEACHES

PEACHES IN SAUTERNES

This is so refreshing, totally delicious and perfumed. Delectably chilled, it makes me want to sing. La!

Don't make this pudding unless the peaches or nectarines are of a very high quality.

Serves 6

8 firm, ripe peaches

8 fresh unsprayed lavender heads, rinsed
1 unwaxed or well-scrubbed lemon
1 x 37.5cl bottle Sauternes, chilled

Peel the peaches and use a small knife to cut them into neat slices around the stone, discarding the stone. Drop into a suitable serving dish. Push in the rinsed lavender heads.

Peel the lemon rind in 2 or 3 long strips and add to the fruit. Pour over enough wine to cover and gently turn the peaches a couple of times in the fragrant liquid.

Cover and chill for at least 4 hours before serving. Serve with a dollop of crème fraîche.

PICKLED PEACHES

These go very well with good slices of cold pink ham or one of those very strong Cheddars that ravage the roof of the mouth.

Makes 2 x 500ml jars

6 firm, ripe peaches
2 small banana shallots
2 long red chillies
600g caster sugar

500ml good-quality red wine vinegar
3 dried bay leaves
10 black peppercorns
2 teaspoons black mustard seeds
2 teaspoons coriander seeds

To sterilise the jars, preheat the oven to 180°C/350°F/Gas 4. Wash 2 good-quality preserving jars and lids really well, removing the rubber seals. Put them on a baking sheet in the oven for 10 minutes.

Meanwhile, cut the peaches in half and remove the stones if you can. Put the peach halves in a large saucepan and just cover with water. Bring to the boil, then remove from the heat and drain the peaches in a colander under cold running water. Peel the peach halves – if they are perfectly ripe, the skin should slip off between your fingers. For more stubborn skin, you may have to resort to a vegetable peeler, but be tender with them, as peaches damage easily. Remove any stones that you weren't able to hoick out first time round.

Cut the shallots in half, then peel and slice them thinly and neatly. Thinly slice the chillies without removing the seeds. Put the shallots and chillies in a large saucepan and add the sugar, vinegar, bay leaves, peppercorns and mustard and coriander seeds. Heat gently until the sugar dissolves.

Add the peaches to the pan and increase the heat. Simmer for 3 minutes, turning them once or twice so they cook evenly. Remove from the heat. Strain the peaches, shallots, chillies, bay leaves and spices through a large sieve, collecting the vinegar syrup in a wide bowl. Pour the syrup back into the pan and bring to the boil. Cook until the liquid has reduced to about 400ml and looks thickened and glossy. It should have the texture of maple syrup. Pour over the peaches.

Spoon the peaches and flavouring ingredients into the 2 warm sterilised jars, ensuring that the shallots, chillies and spices are evenly distributed. Pour the syrup into the jars so that the peaches are fully covered and the jars are almost completely full. Leave to cool for 30 minutes (topping up with more syrup if necessary), then seal the jars and let the peaches sit in a cool, dark place for at least 4 weeks before serving.

GOOSEBERRIES

GOOSEBERRY SNOW

The hairy little gooseberry seems rather forgotten these days. So please revisit this delicious, plump and lonely fruit with this rewarding, snowy-topped and very easy pudding.

Makes 4

500g red or green gooseberries
40g unsalted butter, plus extra,
    for greasing

150g caster sugar
2 large free-range eggs
¼ teaspoon vanilla extract

Top and tail the gooseberries and place them in a saucepan with the butter and 50g of the sugar, to taste. Bubble gently for 6–8 minutes until the fruit is softened but not completely turned to mush. Stir occasionally to prevent it from catching on the bottom of the pan. Remove from the heat and leave to cool for 5 minutes.

Preheat the oven to 190°C/375°F/Gas 5. Separate the eggs. Whisk the egg whites in a clean bowl until stiff. You should be able to turn the bowl upside down without the contents falling on to your shoes. Gradually whisk in the remaining 100g sugar, in small amounts, to make a thick, glossy meringue. Whisk in the vanilla extract.

Beat the egg yolks thoroughly into the gooseberry mixture and spoon into 4 x 150ml ramekins or heatproof glass dishes, which you have lightly buttered. Spoon the meringue gently – but generously – on top and place on a baking tray. Bake for 13–15 minutes until the meringue is just set and very lightly browned. Serve hot.

FINISHED!

Val Warner

DRINKS

CITRON PRESSÉ

The mirage of a shimmering citron pressé is the reward that spurred me on through the fearsome heat of long walks with my father in the South of France. When we finally arrived in a local café, dry-lipped, sweating and exhausted, this lemon juice, water and sugar mixture was the most quenching saviour. Perversely, I would leave it in front of me untouched until I could take no more punishment.

Serves 2

2 juicy lemons

ice-cubes
2 heaped teaspoonfuls white caster sugar
fizzy or flat mineral water

Squeeze the lemons and pour over ice in highball glasses. Stir in the sugar and top up with the water. Simple but amazing. For Dad's version, replace the sugar with a good sprinkling of salt and use fizzy water, then watch it erupt all over the table before you drink it.

OLD-FASHIONED LEMON- AND LIMEADE

If citron pressé seems too basic for you, here's a lemonade that requires a little more exertion. A fine refreshment post barn-raising to drink on the veranda with Ma, Pa and the boys.

Makes 1.5 litres

6 large unwaxed or well-scrubbed lemons
6 large unwaxed or well-scrubbed limes

1 litre water
1kg granulated sugar
25g tartaric acid
fizzy mineral water, to taste

Wash the lemons and limes, then peel the rind in long strips. Put the rind with the water in a saucepan and simmer, lid on, for 15 minutes.

Squeeze the fruit and pour through a fine sieve into the pan. Simmer for 15 minutes with the lid firmly on. Add the sugar and simmer for a further 5 minutes, again with the lid on. Remove from the heat, cool for a few minutes, then stir in the tartaric acid. Allow to sit for at least 3 hours at room temperature before decanting into sterilised bottles (*see* page 161). Mix with fizzy mineral water to taste.

CLASSIC MARGARITA

Why did the Mexican take his wife to the edge of the cliff? Tequila!

There are many disguises for margarita, but for me it is simply sugar syrup, lime juice and tequila. I don't like ice cubes invading my glass; if the drink has been properly chilled in the shaker, I will have drunk it long before it becomes room temperature. I can't really argue the salt; it's a question of taste, but I like it. And tequila is proper tequila only if it is made of 100 per cent blue agave cactus.

One measure is 25ml and this is enough for a cocktail shaker, but you can multiply it for any number using the same proportions.

Makes 2

1 lime wedge
ground sea salt
2 measures freshly squeezed lime juice
6 cubes of ice

4 measures white (blanco) tequila
2 measures sugar syrup (see below)

SUGAR SYRUP
100g caster sugar
200ml water

To make the sugar syrup, dissolve the sugar in the water over a low heat and leave to cool.

Take your martini glass or small tumbler and run a lime wedge around the rim. Upend the glass and press lightly on a small side plate of ground sea salt. Turn it the right way up and attend to the mixing.

Squish the limes on a squeezer, or through a sieve, as you will need to measure it and avoid pips. Fill the cocktail shaker with the ice. Pour over the tequila, sugar syrup and freshly squeezed lime juice. Do not use instant lime juice: BAD!

Put on the cap of the cocktail shaker and shake vigorously 15 times. Remove the cap and pour. Drink immediately, but not in one go.

STUMBLING TORCH (SCRUMPY WITH ELDERFLOWER)

This cooler was discovered in a tent in Kent. It's all my trusty cold-box had left within – apart from some cachaça, which no one fancied. Because of the sweet ease with which this slips down, I suggest that it is best drunk near home, or one tends to have to disappear for yet another night-time hedgerow wee – hence the name! I suggest good, flat, dry farmyard scrumpy or cider.

Serves 4, then 3, then 2, then 1

elderflower cordial (*see* page 214)

ice
1 x battered 2-litre milk container full
 of cider

In a tin mug or beaker, pour a spilling-over capful of elderflower cordial on to 2 cubes of ice. Splash over about 150ml scrumpy or cider, and stir briefly. Drink with a cold sausage in the other hand.

BICYCLETTE

The great British chef Fergus Henderson got me on to this drink of Campari and wine. If I remember correctly, we also added fizzy mineral water. As he would say, 'What a treat!'. And this is just so, for those hot, lazy garden afternoons when it's really hard to lift a finger unless holding one of the following bottles.

1 bottle Campari
1 bottle dry white wine

1 bottle fizzy mineral water

In a highball glass, mix 1 measure Campari (25ml) with ½ glass of wine (75ml) and top up with fizzy mineral water. Drink, then repeat until you've had enough.

ICED COFFEE

Hot coffee seems correct at breakfast, but out of place as the hot day wears on. This is where the iced coffee truly comes into its own. Be careful though: because it's so delicious, you could easily drink too many and then your eyes would pop out and roll through the croquet hoops, and minutes later you would explode.

Serves 2

2 shots of espresso coffee
1 teaspoon unsweetened cocoa powder

2 tablespoons coffee essence,
    such as Camp Coffee
6–8 ice cubes
300ml fridge-cold whole milk

Pour the espresso into a jug and stir in the cocoa powder and coffee essence until smooth. Put the ice cubes in a clean tea-towel and bash with a rolling pin to break into chunky pieces.

Half-fill 2 tall glasses with the ice and pour over the coffee mixture. Top up with the cold milk and serve.

MINT TEA

Being of a fidgety nature, sitting still is difficult. I love endless little excursions. Vis-à-vis office work, the devil on my shoulder comes in the vision of mint tea. The computer is deserted and out the door I am again, sitting in the Moroccan café sipping this sweet distraction.

Tea for 2

2 heaped teaspoons gunpowder green tea
a small bunch of mint, plus 2 sprigs for
the glasses
4 teaspoons caster sugar

If it's a proper tea glass it will have a plastic or metal cradle with a handle. If not, diagonally fold over a paper napkin into a triangle, then wrap it around the glass and twist the ends to secure it.

Heat the kettle, but switch it off just before it comes to the boil. I have come to learn that tea should not be scalded. Brew the tea in a teapot with the mint and sugar. Leave to stand for 2–3 minutes. Stuff an extra sprig of mint into each glass and pour over the tea.

Although this version echoes the absurdly sweet Moroccan tooth, sprinkle in what sugar you will. Goes very well with another Moroccan accompaniment – a cigarette.

INDEX

THANKS TO...

Howard, Scoo dal shalamash jub da jaya oo fed amalish; only you know what that means.

Hattie, your clarity is that of the finest aspic.

Justine, you're a brick – no, you're a rock; I can't thank you enough.

My dear friend Sarah O'Keefe, for her excellent eye and warm heart.

Becca, thank you for making me laugh all the time to the point where I have to get away from you.

Caz, well for just being damn cool.

Grainne Fox, you're the bee's knees; no more bad Irish accents, I promise.

Fiona, for being such fun – love and corkscrews.

Pene, for your cool head.

Peter Hunt, you're a visionary.

Jock, for being a pillar of strength.

Jane for all the too-ing and fro-ing.

June Summerill and Bernadette Bishop, for being smashing.

Diana Henry, you're ace – thanks for your encouragement, endless ciggies, kitchen, and general lack of utensils.

David Lamb, for your interest and kind soul.

Alison and everyone at Mitchell Beazley; what a great company.

Everyone at Optomen, especially Pat and Ben.

Love to the A team – Paul 'isn't it?' Ratcliffe, Gary 'soothing' Broadhurst, Richard 'don't touch my tripod' Hill, Rex 'da pun' Phillips and Faye 'HIYAAA!' Donaldson.

Special thanks and gratitude to all the contributors.

Once again to all my friends and family, Kitty and Cooper, the SEC, and anyone I have accidentally left out.